# *Open Doors*

## VIETNAM POWs THIRTY YEARS LATER

# *Open Doors*

## VIETNAM POWs THIRTY YEARS LATER

JAMIE HOWREN

TAYLOR BALDWIN KILAND

Potomac Books, Inc.
Washington, D.C.

**Library of Congress Cataloging-in-Publication Data**
Kiland, Taylor Baldwin, 1966-
  Open doors : Vietnam POWs thirty years later / Taylor Baldwin Kiland, Jamie Howren.— 1st ed.
      p. cm.
  Includes bibliographical references and index.
  ISBN 1-57488-969-9 (pbk. : alk. paper)—ISBN 1-59797-020-4 (hardcover : alk. paper)
  1. Vietnamese Conflict, 1961-1975—Prisoners and prisons, North Vietnamese. 2. Prisoners of war—United States—Biography. 3. Prisoners of war—Vietnam—Biography. I. Howren, Jamie, 1966- II. Title.

DS559.4.K55 2005
959.704'37'092273—dc22

                                        2005018658

Printed in the United States of America on acid-free paper that meets the American National Standards Institute Z39-48 Standard.

Potomac Books, Inc.
22841 Quicksilver Drive
Dulles, Virginia 20166

First Edition


10  9  8  7  6  5  4  3  2  1

This book is lovingly dedicated to
all those U.S. prisoners of war from Vietnam
who paid the ultimate sacrifice.

"What Epictetus [told] his students was that there can be no such thing
as being the 'victim' of another. You can only be a 'victim' of *yourself*.
It's all how you discipline your mind."

—Vice Adm. James Bond Stockdale, philosopher, naval officer, leader,
actor, son, husband, father, grandfather, inspiration
December 23, 1923 – July 5, 2005

The credit belongs to the man who is actually in the arena . . .
who at the best knows in the end the great triumph of high achievement,
and who at the worst, if he fails, at least fails while daring greatly, so that
his place shall never be with those cold and timid souls
who know neither victory nor defeat.
—Theodore Roosevelt


Freedom suppressed and again regained bites with keener fangs
than freedom never endangered.
—Cicero

# Contents

FOREWORD *IX*
*Joe Galloway*

A SECOND CHANCE AT FREEDOM *XI*
*Ross Perot*

PREFACE *XIII*

**OPEN DOORS:**
VIETNAM POWs THIRTY YEARS LATER   *1*

THE THIRTY   *3*

BIOGRAPHICAL INFORMATION   *91*

WHO ARE THE VIETNAM POWs?   *151*

ACKNOWLEDGMENTS AND HOST VENUES   *168*

INDEX   *176*

ABOUT THE AUTHORS   *184*

# *Foreword*

*T*heir homecoming more than three decades ago was cause for a joyous American national celebration. Some of them had been held prisoner in Vietnam, tortured and brutalized, for more than eight years.

That homecoming in 1973 was something all Americans could cheer, no matter where they stood in a nation deeply divided over the war. It was the only good news out of Vietnam in a long time.

We shared, briefly and tearfully, their televised reunions with their families—families changed by years of absence. There were children who barely remembered a father who had been neither alive nor dead to them for years. There were wives made stronger by the demands of taking care of a family and working to free a husband held prisoner. There were wives who had given up hope and moved on.

We know what happened to some of them. Jeremiah Denton and John McCain were elected to the U.S. Senate. Sam Johnson was elected to the U.S. House of Representatives. Doug Peterson served as the first U.S. Ambassador to the Socialist Republic of Vietnam. Vice Adm. James Stockdale ran for vice president unsuccessfully. Some wrote books about their experiences as POWs. One took his own life only four months after he returned home.

Most simply concentrated on rebuilding lives, personal and professional, that had been put on hold for so long.

How are they doing today? What are they doing today? This book goes a long way toward answering those questions about thirty of the former POWs who came home from Hanoi so long ago.

Two talented young women, writer Taylor Baldwin Kiland and photographer Jamie Howren, who have been friends since childhood, believed that there was a story to tell about these brave men and their lives today, and they set out to tell it.

They put their own savings into the project, visiting thirty former prisoners of war to capture the images and gather the stories that in August 2002 became the highly successful traveling exhibit titled Open Doors: Vietnam POWs Thirty Years Later.

Jamie's black-and-white sepia toned images, shot with one camera and one lens, and Taylor's profiles—character studies—show how these men rebuilt their lives after they came home from a season in hell. They make Open Doors an inspirational story of hope, opportunity, and second chances.

The underlying theme of both the exhibit and this book is found in the words of former POW Cdr. Paul Galanti: "There's no such thing as a bad day when you have a door knob on the inside of the door."

For three years, the Open Doors exhibit has traveled America, going to twenty venues and the territory of Guam, and aboard a U.S. Navy ship at sea, the USS *Boxer*. The Museum of History and Art in Coronado, California, manages the traveling exhibit. When Open Doors ends its road tour in 2006, its permanent home will be the Library of Congress in Washington, D.C.

Joseph L. Galloway
April 2005

# A Second Chance at Freedom

*I*n 2002, Jamie Howren and Taylor Baldwin Kiland produced the extraordinary exhibit Open Doors: Vietnam POWs Thirty Years Later, which has touched the hearts of thousands of those fortunate enough to see it at more than twenty venues around the country.

The Open Doors exhibit traveled throughout the United States and was featured on NBC's *Nightly News with Tom Brokaw*, CNN, and *Parade Magazine*. Jamie and Taylor's book will now allow this story to come into every home.

While I could not help being deeply moved by the commitment and heroism of the POWs who were imprisoned in Vietnam for up to nine years, the rich, full lives they have lived after returning to freedom are even more awe-inspiring.

This book gives you an intimate look into the current lives of our POWs thirty years after their return from Vietnam, focusing on how they rebuilt their lives—professionally and personally.

This inspirational story of hope and opportunity that details what these men made of their second chance at freedom can give us all some perspective for our own lives.

We appreciate the efforts Jamie and Taylor made to give these men the recognition and credit they have so richly earned—and for giving us role models to emulate.

To quote former POW Navy Cdr. Paul Galanti, "There's no such thing as a bad day when you have a door knob on the inside of the door."

Ross Perot
April 2005

# Preface

**P**hotographer Jamie Howren and writer Taylor Baldwin Kiland have been lifelong friends since the second grade at St. Agnes School for Girls in Alexandria, Virginia. They first collaborated as a photographer/writer team for a national nonprofit organization, Little Brothers–Friends of the Elderly, which provides volunteer visiting friends to homebound elderly. They worked together on an event that raised more than $50,000 showcasing the organization's clients—isolated seniors—through a series of black-and-white portraits and text profiles.

When Taylor volunteered for the McCain for President effort in 2000, she met a number of the POWs who were campaigning on behalf of Senator McCain. She was struck by the dearth of information on where these men had been since their release from captivity. With a few notable exceptions, these men had quietly faded back into society. Where were they now and how had they rebuilt their lives after serving as the longest-held group of POWs in our nation's history? Jamie and Taylor decided to showcase—in pictures and words—the paths these men took. They created a museum exhibit of their work, and this book is based on that exhibit.

All interviews and portrait sessions were conducted simultaneously in the subjects' homes, offices, or favorite outdoor locations. The meetings took place between May 2001 and July 2002. Each photograph was taken with a medium-format, Hasselblad camera, using one lens, ambient light, and black-and-white film. The photographer and writer developed each story angle and chose each portrait together, with care taken to ensure the two were complementary.

Separately, the individual profile and portrait give the observer a glimpse at a man. Together, they give insight into how he ticks, how he thinks, and how he lives. The portrait of Capt. Ev Southwick laughing and playing the ukulele gives a visual image of a flirtatious, playful, fun-loving man. However, his profile reveals a much more intimate sense at how laughter has sustained him through three divorces and a brain aneurysm. Not a deeply religious man, he uses laughter as a spiritual release, and the portrait captures his own personal therapy in action.

*Open Doors: Vietnam POWs Thirty Years Later* suggests hope, opportunity, and second chances—a testament to the sheer strength of the human spirit and the power of human will.

As two thirty-something women, we were too young to have served in Vietnam. But we recognized that the history books, the documentary producers, and the writers who have covered the Vietnam experience have overlooked "the rest of the story." We knew there were significant life lessons in how the POWs conducted themselves when they came home. The stories we uncovered were unbelievably moving and so valuable for people of our generation and younger. These men teach us that it is possible to overcome adversity and pursue life, liberty, and happiness—how wonderfully and uniquely American are their stories!

Thank you to all thirty featured in this book (and the countless others who provided support and encouragement) for letting us into your homes and your lives so that we could get a better sense of who you are as men: as husbands, sons, neighbors, coworkers, brothers, fathers, and grandfathers.

As Einstein said, "In the service of life, sacrifice becomes grace." These are the most graceful men we know.

Jamie Howren

Taylor Baldwin Kiland

**Everyone Sang**

Everyone suddenly burst out singing;
And I was filled with such delight
As prisoned birds must find in freedom,
Winding wildly across the white
Orchards and dark-green fields; on—on—and out
   of sight.
Everyone's voice was suddenly lifted;
And beauty came like the setting sun;
My heart was shaken with tears; and horror
Drifted away . . . O, but Everyone
Was a bird; and the song was wordless; the singing will
   never be done.
—Siegfried Sassoon, World War I soldier poet, written in 1919

*The POWs cheer as the AC-141A that ferries them home takes off from Hanoi on February, 12, 1973.* Photo courtesy of the Department of Defense.

# Open Doors: Vietnam POWs Thirty Years Later

*M*en who grew up too young to fight in World War II saw their fathers tested physically and mentally by war. This generation of men had a tremendous sense of faith instilled in them at a very early age—faith in the unwavering loyalty and indomitable bonds of the nuclear family, faith in their government, and faith in their country.

The Vietnam conflict shattered that faith for a generation of youth, but mostly for those who did not serve in uniform. For the aviators captured and held as POWs, time stood still. For the most part, these men did not experience the unrest, the cultural and spiritual conflict our country witnessed during that tumultuous season. *They* never lost their faith in our system, but clung to it—some might say naively. Regardless, it sustained them and empowered them.

Aviators are known for pushing the limits of physics and for cheating fate. They signed up for Vietnam to be tested. In their profession, they couldn't afford to be ambivalent or to lose their convictions.

What happened when their dignity and independence were stripped away in a prison in North Vietnam? They survived.

Collectively, they endured out of a fear of losing their dignity. They felt an innate sense of obligation to do what was right in the eyes of their fellow prisoners and to show honor to their country. It was never a solitary struggle, as each of them supported and validated the others. It constantly motivated them.

Perhaps that is what is missing in younger generations—the fear of shame, the sense of sacrifice as the ultimate grace.

Some prisoners or victims of unfortunate fates wallow in self-pity, some reflect on their lives and opportunities lost. Some lose their faith; some gain a renewed sense of spirituality. For those whose fate dictated that they spend precious personal and professional years in torturous isolation in North Vietnam, there were two choices: self-destruction or a search of their inner core and a beseeching of their Maker for the patience to tolerate their captors and simply endure: Get through each day, one day at a time. Get out mentally and physically intact. Return with their names and reputations whole.

Most POWs from the Vietnam era do not brood on the fortunes or misfortunes resulting from the conflict and their imprisonment. Few wallow in the "What ifs?" of their lives. Is this a particularly masculine trait? Can it be attributed to military training or to values instilled in them as children? Did it play a significant role in their mental health and in the resurrection of their lives upon their return? What is it about the will of these men that makes them so extraordinary?

These men were not given celebrity treatment by today's standards, nor did they seek it. They weren't given book deals or movie deals or publicists or a million dollars. Rather, they were asked to resume their roles as husbands, fathers, and sons and to salvage their careers. Some families survived; others broke apart. But the men didn't. Most have flourished. None of them would claim to be perfect, but they refuse to be bitter, and they take great pride in their individual accomplishments. Most relish life, for they know that God understands them intimately and that life always presents new doors of opportunity to open. Peel away the layers and you'll find strong fiber at their core. Take a look at where life has taken them—or, more appropriately, where they've taken their lives.

# The Thirty

The Honorable Everett Alvarez Jr., Commander, USN (Ret.)   4

Colonel William D. Beekman, USAF (Ret.)   7

Commander George T. Coker, USN (Ret.)   10

Lieutenant Colonel Thomas E. Collins III, USAF (Ret.)   13

Captain Render Crayton, USN (Ret.)   16

Colonel George E. "Bud" Day, USAF (Ret.)   19

The Honorable Jeremiah A. Denton Jr., Rear Admiral, USN (Ret.)   22

Captain John C. "Jack" Ensch, USN (Ret.)   25

Captain John H. Fellowes, USN (Ret.)   28

Commander Paul E. Galanti, USN (Ret.), and Mrs. Phyllis Galanti   31

Mr. Douglas B. Hegdahl   34

Captain James L. "Duffy" Hutton, USN (Ret.)   37

The Honorable Samuel R. Johnson, U.S. House of Representatives
and Colonel, USAF (Ret.)   40

Floyd Harold "Hal" Kushner, MD, FACS, Colonel, USA (Ret.)   43

Vice Admiral William P. Lawrence, USN (Ret.)   46

Lieutenant Colonel Tony Marshall, USAF (Ret.)   49

Vice Admiral Edward H. Martin, USN (Ret.)   52

The Honorable John S. McCain, U.S. Senator and Captain, USN (Ret.),
and the Honorable Orson G. Swindle III   55

Captain John Michael McGrath, USN (Ret.)   58

Major General Edward J. Mechenbier, USAF (Ret.)   61

Captain Ernest M. "Mel" Moore Jr., USN (Ret.)   64

Captain Richard D. "Moon" Mullen, USN (Ret.), and Mrs. Peggy Mullen   67

Colonel Ben M. Pollard, USAF (Ret.)   69

Brigadier General Robinson Risner, USAF (Ret.), and Mrs. Dorothy Risner   72

Major Wesley D. Schierman, USAF (Ret.)   75

Captain Edwin A. Shuman III, USN (Ret.)   78

Captain C. Everett Southwick, USN (Ret.)   81

Vice Admiral James Bond Stockdale, USN (Ret.), and Mrs. Sybil Stockdale   83

Captain Richard A. Stratton, USN (Ret.), and granddaughters
Allyson, Ashley, and Amanda   85

The Honorable Orson G. Swindle III, Federal Trade Commissioner and
Lieutenant Colonel, USMC (Ret.)   88

# On His Own

## THE HONORABLE EVERETT ALVAREZ JR., COMMANDER, USN (RET.)

**W**hat was it like being one of the first? Ev Alvarez responds with dead-pan wit and a mischievous smile on his face: "Somebody had to do the advance work."

"Being the first has its positives and its not so positives. Especially when I speak to women's groups and I'm introduced as the first guy shot down [and held] for eight and a half years. The ladies in the audience exclaim, 'Ohhh!' And I wonder, why didn't this happen when I was in high school?" He pauses to get a reaction from his audience. "I think I'm gonna use that one [in my next speech]."

Ev wasn't always comfortable being in the spotlight. He describes himself as a generally quiet and shy man, a loner. He developed an ability to compartmentalize, focus, and distract himself based on early childhood experiences. "I think I found it easy because I had learned to live with myself. When you grow up in a turbulent household, you have to learn to shut things out. It was a mechanism for me, a survival technique."

It served him well and, like it or not, he became a role model. As one of the first POWs, Ev was an anomaly. He was the only American POW in Hanoi for the first six months of his captivity. For those who were shot down after him, Ev was an inspiration.

"The best thing I did was just be there. The stories go that [my cell mates] used to say, 'I used to feel sorry for myself, but then I'd look at you.'" The fact that he was still surviving, still fighting, and still sane boosted the spirits of the others who were captured after him. "In their minds, I was still making it. It wasn't anything prophetic I said or heroic I did. I was just . . . there . . . and still playing the game."

In the Navy and in business, Ev has made a reputation for going out on his own, pursuing his own quest for success. What made him venture off on his own? Quite simply, "I got laid off."

A short stint with a private health care company had left him without a job. He had a law degree but had never practiced. But after a career in the Navy and a political appointment in the Department of Veterans Affairs, he knew how to navigate the government bureaucracy. So he started his own business, buying a small federal contracting company with two partners. "My experience had been in government, at various levels. So, I thought that was the front door." Fifteen years later, Conwal Inc. has three hundred employees.

"We're federal government contractors. We provide management support and engineering support to the FAA, the State Department, the Department of

Defense. We compete against Booz Allen and Arthur Andersen. We go after little niche areas—we have very good senior people that keep busy because of their expertise. Engineering, conference management—all over the country and all over the world . . . *it keeps us busy."*

What's made him successful? Without missing a beat and with a gleam in his big, round, doelike eyes, he says, "Charm, smile." One second, two seconds of silence. "Nah—networking, personal relationships—that's what helps. People are looking for someone they can trust to do the work. They have so many people knocking on their doors. Once you know someone, they trust you, so they help you out. You still have to compete for the work, but . . . it's the personal experience of working with a customer or by reputation. We've had our cycle—sometimes it comes easier, sometimes it's tough."

Steady focus, patience, just being there at the right time with the right skills.

# Evergreen

## COLONEL WILLIAM D. BEEKMAN, USAF (RET.)

*H*e fought to get into the action in Vietnam. He fought for career success on his own terms. And now he is fighting multiple sclerosis. But Bill Beekman contin-ues to stand tall, proud, and fearless.

As the valedictorian of his high school class of more than five hundred students, he had his choice of universities and scholarships: the University of Michigan, the University of Virginia, MIT, and Purdue. But he wanted to be an astronaut and study astronautical engineering, so he looked at the service academies. He came in first place on his service exam, so his local congressman said, "Which academy would you like an appointment to?"

He found himself at the U.S. Air Force Academy, where he loved the academics. Graduating in 1968 at the height of the conflict, Bill fully expected he would go to Vietnam, and he wanted to be in the action. After pilot training and two stateside assignments flying the F-4 Phantom, Bill practically begged to go to Vietnam. He finally landed a combat fighter assignment in Danang, and the flying was fantastic. "We lived and breathed the war because we would fly South Vietnam missions, Laos, North Vietnam, and Cambodia. And we flew every type of mission there was." He was shot down in June 1972 on his 175th mission and held until repatriation in March 1973.

Diagnosed with multiple sclerosis in 1987, Bill refuses to let it dictate his lifestyle. But his illness did make active duty in the Pentagon too physically demanding, so he retired from the Air Force as a colonel. He returned to his adopted home-town of Dayton, Ohio, with his wife and two children and went to work for defense contractor Booz Allen Hamilton, but, again, his illness hindered his career path.

So Bill started his own company with a high school friend. They called it Pulma Labs, and it served a niche within the medical industry that no one else was serving: pulmonary function testing, evaluating the oxygen needs of Medicare patients in their homes. After a few years of entrepreneurial struggle, companies started calling from all over the country. The business expanded, with district offices in several states and annual revenues in excess of $2 million. Bill and his partner were working sixty to eighty hours a week. How did that affect his health? "It really didn't, and maybe it's because I'm one of those people who strives, who thrives on crisis management."

Bill recently sold Pulma Labs. "A group of physicians made us an offer we

couldn't refuse." But he still serves on the company's board of directors and offers his advice to the current owners.

MS has slowed Bill down physically. It has severely affected his ability to walk and has even impaired his vocal chords. But he fights the disease every day: he swims thirty laps three days a week, lifts weights, uses a stationary bike, and visits a medical massage therapist about once a week. And it was his masseuse who introduced him to his current wife, Donna, a woman he describes as "just perfect for me. We live for today and we like to go and do! . . . She looked right past the illness."

His next challenge? To compete in a swim meet at his local YMCA. "They don't have a category for disabilities, so I'm going to have to compete in my age group with everybody else. I want to race in the 200M or 400M freestyle, so I'll have to build up my endurance and speed." Steadfastly and consistently, Bill continues to find new ways to strive, to grow, and to prosper. He's hearty and not easily broken. "When you've been through the worst, you feel you can do anything."

# *The Kid*

## COMMANDER GEORGE T. COKER, USN (RET.)

Reckless or courageous? As they crawled through the rice paddies outside of Hanoi miles away from freedom and only a few miles from the prison, George McKnight (the older George) stopped and looked at George Coker (the younger George) and said, "You know, George, someday you're going to have a helluva story to tell your grandkids." And he went back to crawling through the paddies.

George Coker laughs now, but the escape attempt went down in the history books as one of the most daring. Their idea involved slowly cutting away the lock on their prison door, climbing over the prison wall, crawling through the night shadows of the streets of Hanoi, and wading through the rice paddies to a riverbank. Then they stripped to their underwear and floated downstream all night, hoping to eventually reach friendly forces at the river's mouth. They were discovered the next morning as they tried to find cover from the hot and glaring sun. "It was fun while it lasted," he laments.

George is legendary for his adventures. He says he was always the type who pushed the limits with his parents. One summer during college at Rutgers University, he decided to hitchhike across country with only a quarter in his pocket. He traveled from his home in New Jersey south to Mississippi, then across Texas and New Mexico, then north to Utah—where he worked on a sheep ranch. From there, he headed to Seattle to visit his brother and then continued on through Montana, Indiana, Pennsylvania—all the while earning his ticket back to New Jersey. He said he had a few hairy incidents: he was propositioned (and not by a woman) and threatened, but he says he never feared for his life.

Was he daring or foolish? That is open to interpretation. But his sense of independence and adventure certainly helped him survive in Vietnam as an aviator and as a captive. He is also somewhat of a loner, someone who prefers to

**10**

spend quiet time at home with his wife, Pam, whom he met a few months after returning from Vietnam. He likes to work around the house and build miniature ship models, a hobby he finds exciting. Pam says, "If he has a choice to go to a cocktail party or work on a model, he'd be working on a model."

"You're actually constructing something and there are hundreds of pieces to it." Pointing to a model, he explains, "These were all two-foot pieces of wood, fairly thin, and you gotta cut the planks yourself. The *Victory* I got is really a mini ship. Ships like that take about two thousand hours. This here took several hundred hours. I remember doing the hull on a temporary duty trip to Coronado.

I took the model with me and worked on it. I was trying to put the hull together. I would watch TV at night. It would only take me five minutes to put the plank on, but then it had to be held in place until the glue set . . . so every commercial I would put a plank on and then I would watch a movie for fifteen minutes and hold it. It took me about three nights . . . one plank every fifteen minutes. That's what it takes to get it done."

Not many would have that kind of patience. But perhaps it is a skill he honed in Vietnam. Silently, patiently, and methodically, he and George McKnight plotted and waited for that split second of opportunity to escape. As one of the youngest of the POWs—he was 23 when he was shot down, George was the kid brother. "The attitude was just like a family growing up. They used to say to me, 'That's a good idea. George, you're the youngest, you go do it.'" And so he did.

Recently retired from his job as a computer analyst for the government, he and Pam, now empty nesters, plan to drive across country and visit old friends. They are looking forward to spending time together and to their civic activities. "We've had a good life, so we're gonna give some of it back." He plans to stay active in their church and as a Boy Scout master for a local troop.

What does he like about scouting? "The character building and leadership development. . . . I was big into scouting when I was a kid and it probably saved my life over in Vietnam. . . . I went through one of the worst torture series and it went on for about two months. . . . They were trying to break me and they got me to a point where I was totally exhausted after four or five weeks of standing up with my arms held over my head for eighteen hours a day. . . . It became a mental battle to keep going and keep fighting back. [At that point,] I had long since forgotten my family and names and schools and things like that. The last thing I was holding onto was just the beginning of the Scout oath: 'On my honor, I'll do my best.' It would take me about a minute to get that phrase into my mind . . . and then I would do it again. I had learned [the oath] early and [scouting] was a good experience [for me.] It represented so much to me . . . that was the last tiny thing I could hold onto." Finally, the torturers quit or he won—he doesn't remember which. Helluva story to tell the grandkids.

# Snap Beans

## Lieutenant Colonel Thomas E. Collins III, USAF (Ret.)

*T*om Collins's family has been firmly rooted in Mississippi for at least five generations. They have owned thousands of acres of local land, harvesting pine trees, selling oil, and raising cattle. And they have grown, preserved, and passed down a pure breed variety of snap bean seed since the 1700s. This particular bean is the sacred family nectar.

"It's been in the family for years and years and years . . . [from] my mutha's side of the family since the mid-1700s. . . . And they're not hybrid, they're the original seed. They're not doctored up and tinkered with. . . . You cain't freeze them or anything. Just pull 'em and eat 'em. . . . A nice fresh one that's pulled from the garden—it is delicious!"

On his own acre of land in his backyard near Meridian, he cultivates a plentiful garden of day lilies, grapes, roses, gladiolas, peppers, tomatoes, muscodine vines, pink magnolias, plum trees, and Rose of Sharon trees. "I probably have a hundred kinds of plants around here." Tom relishes being outside in the sunshine. "When Tom is not in his office, he's in the yard," says his wife, Donnie. "When you think about being shut away for seven years, four months, and two weeks. . . . He just loves to garden and be outside—he really does." She watches, amused, as he takes deep inhales of the country air before each thought.

Donnie is his childhood sweetheart. "Our back fences adjoined" as kids. They raised two children and have three grandchildren. Like Tom, Donnie is sharp-tongued and full of vim; she is half honey and half vinegar and all southern. She describes their life and their home: "Tom and I, we live kinda simply, grandchildren and odds and ends of stuff. . . . Tom's the busiest retired person you ever met. But we're really kinda simple people." Their lives revolve around their grandchildren's schedules.

One son, a pathologist, who was born two weeks after Tom was captured in

1965, died suddenly at the young age of thirty-four of an apparent of a heart attack induced by hepatitis. A heartbreaking event for Tom and Donnie, the loss was harder for them than the separation they endured in Vietnam. Some couples never recover from the loss of a child, but they have stuck together. Donnie smiles, "Some days we don't even like each other. 'Would you like to get a divorce?' I say." Tom jokingly chimes in, "But I hate lawyers so much, I won't even go talk with them." They both chuckle and look down at the ground when talking about this episode in their life. They shake their heads and seem to shoo away the pain physically. While she likes to stir things up between them, her acid wit also seems to bring the tension back to a com-

fortable level. They seem charmed by each other.

Tom's other love is politics. Although he initially started a real estate development company after retiring from the Air Force, he found his niche in several political positions: as the executive director of a state agency under two governors and as an assistant secretary of labor in the first Bush Administration. Emboldened by his political achievements and in keeping with his penchant for public policy, he made a run for a congressional seat in 1988. "I just have always been interested in world events, politics, but became more so due to my experience in Vietnam. . . . If I had not been [in prison] for seven years and had not had an opportunity to think about it, I might have finished my career as a fighter pilot or with the airlines. But little events in life change the whole direction, you know? And I think having been a POW affected my thinking to the point that I became real interested in political affairs."

He didn't win the election, but he remains somewhat of a state celebrity and is frequently consulted for his opinions on war, veterans' issues, and politics. He is an establishment in southern Mississippi, a well-rooted product of the state, proud of his heritage and accomplishments, resilient, distinctly southern, and crisp with flavor. Kinda like his snap beans.

# *Hard Lessons*

## Captain Render Crayton, USN (Ret.)

*M*y southern roots are a big part of who I am. I believe in people having manners; I open doors for women. And if I tell someone I'm going to do something, I do it. That's the way I was brought up."

Genteel and polished, Render Crayton is a humble soul with a distinct southern drawl. He is divorced, but his ex-wife and grown son live near his home in La Jolla, California. Render's humility was seeded early on as a young boy in the South. He was raised in LaGrange, Georgia, in a large antebellum mansion full of women. With few divorced families in the South in those days, his mother, grandmother, great-grandmother, sister, and maid replaced the traditional nuclear family.

As a single mother with a master's degree, Render's mother was an anomaly. He has tremendous respect for her intellectual curiosity and her pluck. But she was hard on him, encouraging him to strive, and drilling into him her values.

She saw his tremendous potential. She was disappointed when he quit Boy Scouts to join the football team—just before he made Eagle Scout. It's a decision he now regrets. "She was right. You should never quit something when you're so close to achieving it."

She's still kicking at age ninety-eight, and she's still hard on him. There is both reverence and humility in his voice when he describes their relationship. He smiles slightly, looks down toward the floor, and kicks a nearby table leg. "Yeah, she's a tough woman, all right." The lessons she imparted were difficult to learn, but they stuck with him.

"At one point during my captivity, I was taken to a remote camp with about fifty-five people and came to find out through the walls that I was the most senior prisoner in the camp. It was a terrible responsibility. I recall one guy—a

16

Marine who was tougher than nails. They had his arms and legs tied to a stool for days. Some of the guys tapped on the wall and asked me if I would give him permission to give in. I agonized over it and then told them, 'No, I'm not goin' to tell him that. Orson knows when he's ready to give up and nothin' I'm goin' to say is gonna to make a difference.'"

In prison, they all had to get along, but they also knew what was expected of them. Render didn't feel it was up to him to force them to resist; like most southerners, he expected their values to guide them. After he returned from Vietnam, he continued a career in the Navy, including a stint as the commanding

officer of Naval Air Station Rota, Spain, whose image he was instrumental in restructuring. He quietly and calmly did his job; the transformation was subtle, but the results were noticeable. With a distinctive rhythm in their speech, gait, and work style, southerners make an impact—gently, but measurably.

"Southerners aren't dictatorial-type people. I guess my management style is tempered by that. We like to get along. We trust people. In the South and in the Navy, a handshake is as good as a paper document, and that's the way I feel."

# The Crusader

## COLONEL GEORGE E. "BUD" DAY, USAF (RET.)

The eighteen-wheelers whiz along the rural Florida highway, leaving wind wakes in their path, and another blast of heat in the already sultry air. The shingle out front says "Day & Meade, Attorneys at Law." It could pass for a small-town insurance company or a country real estate office. But step inside Bud Day's domain and the sense of activity practically pulsates. It's alive—with piles of books and phone messages on his computer, on his desk, on shelves, and even on the floor. Pictures and mementos of Bud's legendary military feats and his historical legacy frame the walls, giving perspective and credibility to the fight he is waging today.

Almost eighty years old and one of the most highly decorated military officers since Gen. Douglas MacArthur, Bud still retains his handsome and hearty midwestern good looks. He also still maintains the work schedule of someone half his age: he comes to the office six days a week. Doris, his wife of fifty-three years and his childhood sweetheart, comes to the office with him; she handles the books, oversees the office, and answers the phone. She knows how to manage him at home and at work. Born to Norwegian immigrants, Doris has affectionately earned the nickname the "Viking."

Bud and Doris are fighting the cause of his life against an enemy he swore to protect and defend in World War II, in Korea, and in Vietnam: the United States government. He has filed a class action lawsuit against the United States on behalf of military retirees who, having served their country for more than twenty years, have now been forced to pay for their medical benefits through Medicare. For some of his clients on fixed incomes, this is prohibitively expensive. He and his clients claim a simple breach of contract: These retirees were promised free lifetime medical care and retired pay in return for their career

**19**

dedication to this country. In their words, a promise is a promise, and it's been broken. "The government claimed the U.S. never made this agreement, that no one in the government had the authority to make this contract with us and that no statutes ever authorized our medical care. These are outright, bold-faced, ignoble lies."

Bud's interest in the law was sparked at an early age. After a stint as an enlisted Marine in World War II, he returned to his hometown of Sioux City, Iowa, to attend the University of South Dakota law school and to court Doris. He

received an appointment as an officer in the National Guard in 1950 and was subsequently called to active duty in Korea and Vietnam as fighter pilot. His Herculean feats include surviving a no-chute bailout in 1952 and the longest escape and evasion from enemy forces on record for an American POW in Vietnam. He actually survived for more than two weeks in the jungle, crossing into South Vietnam and crawling to within two miles of an American outpost before he was captured again and held prisoner for a total of sixty-seven months. For his heroic escape attempt, he was awarded the Medal of Honor.

After Vietnam and retirement from the Air Force, he opened his own law practice. "The people I represent are particularly poor or disenfranchised or incapable of making sure that they get justice themselves, so that's the kind of cases I do. I've had some years where I made just basically zero money." Why the law? "Well, it's a lot like flying fighters. There's a lot of one-on-one, there's a lot of confrontation in terms of, you know, representing one person, one point of view—it's a theater that I like to operate in."

"There are three million eligible World War II and Korean war retirees and spouses. Thirty thousand die each month. Thousands of our enlisted retirees have no care, or little care. This is criminal and obscene." But the battle Bud has chosen is not going to be an easy one. He successfully appealed the case in the U.S. Court of Appeals in February 2001, but the government is still fighting him. They filed a request for a rehearing in the U.S. Court of Appeals, which was held on March 6, 2002. Bud fully expects the case to go all the way to the Supreme Court. And he intends to win. For this is the crusade of Bud's life. "I'm going to make this work or die in the attempt. And I'm not going to die trying."

# *The Samaritan*

## THE HONORABLE JEREMIAH A. DENTON JR., REAR ADMIRAL, USN (RET.)

He volunteered, even pleaded, to go back. Jerry Denton was distraught that the United States was pulling out of Vietnam and, in his opinion, breaking their promise to the South Vietnamese people—despite military victories on the battlefield. "It was a war situation, but, God, it was a betrayal. We have never done that in our history. Very few nations have copped out like that." The government wouldn't let him return to Vietnam, as all Americans were being evacuated from the country. Was it the fear of defeat? Was it the feeling of wasted effort after spending almost eight years as a POW? "It was a tough experience to see this country torn asunder."

Jerry has always had the fervor and the passion for the causes he believes in. You could call him a zealot. But that moniker wouldn't do him justice. He lives by a simple rule, a golden one, and he wants to be good and do the right thing in the eyes of his Lord. He is admittedly far from a perfect man and perhaps that makes him even more forgiving to others who fall short of the standard he strives to meet. But he never stops seeking it. He is the product of divorced parents and a wayward father who, as Jerry describes him, would "come home drunk, sometimes too drunk. He spent a lot of our money gambling. . . . He was not as responsible as he could have been in conventional ways. But nobody ever disliked him. He was dead honest. . . . He was not a bad man. He was like me."

A devoted and devout Catholic and a diehard political conservative, the one-time fighter pilot, POW and U.S. Senator still has the fire in him, but for more humanitarian aims now. When he was serving in the Senate in the 1980s, he established an international aid program now known as The Denton Program. Under this government initiative, millions of pounds of critical equipment and supplies are shipped to needy people throughout the world on military aircraft—

on a space-available basis and at no cost to donors. Now, he is taking this concept one step further by fighting to get unused relief supplies transported in empty containers on commercial ships and aircraft to places and people in need.

"There's two thousand times more commercial space available than there is military space available—we import ninety times what we export. So, I thought, why not appeal to those guys and see if they'll allot space available because there's so much of it? . . . The hindrance [for charitable organizations] is the cost of oceanic transportation. It's prohibitive. Sometimes it exceeds the value of the

property you're taking." Take the oversupply in this country to places of equally high demands in other countries. Sounds simple enough. But it hasn't been, for it requires convincing one transportation company at a time and even changing some laws—all from his small office in Mobile, Alabama. "This is the biggest deal I've ever done in my life and I thank God for it."

Jerry has many visions of the way the world should be. He takes a deep drag on his cigarette, closes his eyes, and wildly gesticulates as he pontificates. "It's very simple. You love God unreservedly. And you love your neighbors as you love yourself. Who's your neighbor? It's half the world that doesn't have a damn thing. . . . We have figured out a practical way to manifest love . . . that will lift the poor from where they are to self-sustenance. . . . The water lifts everybody."

# *Feeling Whole*

## CAPTAIN JOHN C. "JACK" ENSCH, USN (RET.)

*J*ack Ensch's wife, his college sweetheart, has become an avid San Diego Padres fan. "Before I got this job, Kathy thought a hit and run was leaving the scene of an accident; now she questions every move a manager makes. 'You know, why didn't he bunt, why didn't he hit and run? Make him steal! Change the pitcher!' She's become a real fan of the game, which is really nice since I'm now doing this for a living."

Jack is director of military marketing for the San Diego Padres, the only Major League Baseball team to have a position dedicated to serving the military market. Like most Americans, he got his first taste of baseball as a kid. "I remember going to my first baseball game with my uncle in the St. Louis, Missouri, Sportsman Park. I first went to see the St. Louis Browns play and later the Cardinals. Driving down there in the late 1940s or early 1950s, going down to the ballpark, sitting in the stands with peanuts and a hot dog. . . . It was just very memorable. I can remember the smell and the sights and the sounds and it was just very exciting. However, I didn't get to go to that many games as a youth because we didn't have much money. I had to rely on the radio."

Jack's father was a factory worker in Springfield, Illinois, and his mother was a waitress. Neither had a college degree, but they raised him to place a premium on family and education. Jack has a master's degree, a thirty-seven-year marriage, three college-educated daughters, and two grandchildren. He proudly considers these his greatest accomplishments.

As a midwesterner, Jack is easygoing and friendly and replete with patriotic pride. But being shot down and losing a thumb in Vietnam took away some of his ego. Injured during his jet ejection, his thumb was amputated without anesthesia. The incident earned him the nickname "Fingers." For a long time, he was self-conscious about it. "I was frustrated that I couldn't do things that I had

been able to do before—and I guess I was feeling sorry for myself as well—
'Why me? It's not fair.' I just didn't want to be looked upon as a cripple, I guess.
The macho fighter aviator mentality was fogging my thinking." His younger
brother, Leon, snapped him out of it. "He said, 'Get your damn hand out of
your pocket. You have nothing to be ashamed of for your injury.'"

That was the wake-up call. Jack figured out a way to wrap his hand so he
could play handball again and he took up long-distance running again, eventually finishing ten marathons. He also returned to flight status and was able to fly
jets again. Being back in the game physically boosted his spirits mentally. It
made him feel whole again.

At the Padres, he's been an inspiration to the young staff members who work with him. "I've been told by many of the young men and women I've worked with here that they have learned from me. Things like integrity, honesty, teamwork . . . keeping a sense of humor. And, yes, I've learned from some of them, too. . . . Just because I'm older doesn't mean I have all the answers."

Targeting the military market is smart for the Padres, given the large military community in San Diego. Since Jack has been with the Padres, attendance by military fans has increased by 5 to 10 percent. "The Padres is a good organization. I'm the old dinosaur among them, but there are a lot of young people here who are very enthusiastic about baseball and are having a good time. They are hard workers and they put in a lot of long hours—not unlike sailors in the fleet in a lot of ways."

The job fills him up, fuels his need to be involved, to stay on the field, and to get up to bat. "There's always something new and different and I feel like I'm still doing something worthwhile for the military and their families." It keeps him active and offers a fitting finale for a man whose career has been devoted to service. He shrugs and squints to make his words more pointed. "Everyone thinks the POW experience was the end. It's not. It was just the beginning."

# The Icebreaker

## CAPTAIN JOHN H. FELLOWES, USN (RET.)

*I* maintained that if you don't have a sense of humor, you better give it up. Because there's too many things that go on in life that you can take too seriously. But if you take it seriously, you can drag yourself into a little knot. So, why don't you laugh a little bit?" Jack Fellowes is a jokester, but he means it when he talks about the importance of maintaining a sense of humor. Laughing and making jokes broke the tension in prison life and helped to boost everyone's spirits.

Jackie Fe, as his friends call him, is a nickname that was coined by his North Vietnamese captors. "Fe" is the chemical symbol for iron—an appropriate one for a man who survived more than six and a half years in Hanoi and lost the use of his arms for thirteen months. "I went through a little bit of grieving at first, but then I got over it quickly. . . . Of course, Ron [Bliss, my prison roommate] would tell me stories and make me laugh. I'd laugh so hard my [broken] arms would hurt. So, I'd tell him, 'Don't make me laugh anymore!'" But Jack didn't really mean it; the laughing actually helped him to heal.

Jack is the type of guy who puts everyone at ease. At a social gathering, he's the one who mingles first. "I shake hands with everyone. I say, 'Hey, I'm Jack Fellowes. This is my wife, Pat.'" Some would call him approachable and easygoing; some might call him the classic class clown. He's a guy's guy; he has a husky demeanor mixed with humility and disarming charm. He's solidly down to earth and his self-deprecating style draws people to him. And, of course, he is drawn to anyone who can make him laugh. His favorite comedian is Red Skelton. Why? "Because everything he says is just plain funny! He doesn't need to use foul language in his jokes."

When Jack left for Vietnam, he and Pat had four young children. The youngest, Tom, was only two years old when Jack was shot down. But Pat never let them forget their dad and made his presence ubiquitous. She even kept a picture of Jack on the breakfast table.

28

On his first night home from captivity, when he was recuperating at Portsmouth Naval Hospital in Virginia, he saw his children for the first time. "When I left, they were two, four, six, and eight. When I came home, they were nine, eleven, thirteen, and fifteen." They walked into his hospital room and "there they were. Tom had a hat on, a baseball cap with a long brim, so I couldn't see his face. They all wanted to talk, but Tom never said a word. He just sat there. As they were walking out, I said to Pat, 'What's wrong with Tom? He's not speaking.' She said, typical Pat, 'Well, you've bee gone a long time. Give him a chance.' Tom got to the door. Everyone had gone. He puts his head way back, looked at

me from under his hat and says, 'Dad, you're the greatest.' I was floored. It makes me cry now." Jack's penetrating eyes get just a little misty recounting the story and his voice falters a bit. Perhaps this was the greatest test of his ability to put people at ease. And it still makes him proud.

Since he retired from the Navy after thirty years of service, Jack has stayed active—at Pat's insistence. "My wife let me retire for about twelve minutes. She said, 'What are you doing home?' And I made the mistake that I guess a lot of husbands make. I said, 'I live here.' And she said, 'Not during the day.'" So he works at the Maryland State Legislature as a liquor inspector, as an auxiliary policeman, and as a judge in county elections.

Jack still thinks people take life too seriously. A lobbyist at the State Legislature asked Jack if he worked there. In a typical deadpan comment, he responded, "Why would I be standing behind this counter if I didn't work here? Actually, I have two jobs. In the afternoons, I go downstairs to the phone booth and become Superman." The woman stared at him blankly. He huffs a bit and says, "You could just feel the joke swish right over her head. I could see it brush her hair."

# *The Activists*

## COMMANDER PAUL E. GALANTI, USN (RET.), AND MRS. PHYLLIS GALANTI

A t a White House state dinner for the POWs in 1973, then–Secretary of State Henry Kissinger looked at Paul Galanti, then looked at Phyllis Galanti, then looked at Paul again and said to him in his famous accent and with a chuckle, "Your vife: she caused me so much trouble . . . "

After Paul was shot down and captured, Phyllis moved to Richmond, Virginia. She wanted to be near her parents who had retired there. She didn't know what her future held and she didn't know a soul in Richmond, but she got a job as a secretary at Reynolds Metals Company and went to work making a life for herself.

The Bring Paul Home campaign, initiated by Phyllis and embraced by her adopted home of Richmond, was long-suffering and did not easily win. Phyllis, Sybil Stockdale, and many POW wives worked tirelessly for their husbands' release, making appeals to Congress, the White House, the State Department—whoever would listen to their case.

Six years later, when Virginia welcomed Paul home with an event at the State Capitol, Phyllis was arguably one of the most famous ladies in the state. Senator Ed Willey, president pro tempore of the State Senate, shared with Paul, "Your little lady was quite a little lady while you were overseas." He proceeded to tell Paul that only two nonlegislators had ever addressed the joint session of the Virginia General Assembly: Robert E. Lee and Phyllis.

The homecoming celebration was a ticker tape parade the likes of which Richmond—not to mention Paul Galanti—had never seen. He was pleasantly surprised at how his shy wife had blossomed into a political activist—all on his behalf. He literally gushes when he talks about her. "Everyone knew her," says Paul. "She did this very high-profile Bring Paul Home campaign, and everyone thought I was from here. The first time I spent any time in Richmond was my welcome home at the State Capitol for five thousand people, and they didn't come to see me. They came to see her."

They reversed roles on the McCain for President campaign when he served as Virginia State Chair and she helped out behind the scenes. "The McCain thing really got me excited," Phyllis admits. Whatever they dedicate themselves to, they both support it.

There is a steadfastness and level of comfort between the two of them that

has made them a formidable and enduring team. They describe each other as very different personalities, but complementary. Phyllis says she's the planner, the list maker; Paul contends that "if you don't plan anything, then nothing goes wrong." According to Paul, Phyllis is the introvert who "gets stuff done"; Paul is the extrovert who just "blows hard." Opposites attract.

Phyllis says that her time alone during the Vietnam War not only made her independent, but empowered her to be and do exactly what she wants. She is quietly forceful and very direct. Paul, on the other hand, is both tender and playful. He is gentle and affectionate, warm and soft to the touch when he shakes a hand or guides an arm. And his eternal optimism was notorious in Vietnam. "I never got down the whole time. . . . Everything was always a good sign." Paul insisted on seeing the glass half full. "You know, the whole time I was there, there was always a lot of stuff that probably should have been serious which [I thought] was funny. I mean, I never laughed in their faces, but some of these guards were funny. . . . Every time I'd look at them in their little mushroom hats, you know, they looked like little mushrooms walking around."

There were a lot of pessimists among the group. One fellow captive said to Paul, "What are you laughing at? Don't you know we're gonna die here?" But Paul remained persistent in his attitude. "From the day I was shot down until the day we went home, I was convinced it would just be another six months . . . " Maybe he also knew subconsciously that Phyllis was not only stoking the home fires, but chipping away at the North Vietnamese resolve, one day at a time.

# *Memorable*

## Mr. Douglas B. Hegdahl

*I* always like the POW reunions 'cause I'm the youngest. At work, I'm the old guy, so I guess it's all relative." Unlike most of his POW colleagues, he wasn't shot down from a jet or captured in the jungles of Vietnam. He was plucked out of the Gulf of Tonkin after falling overboard from his ship where he was a very young and newly minted sailor.

Doug was born near Watertown, South Dakota. His parents were of Scandinavian descent, but they refused to teach the kids Norwegian, insisting Doug and his two brothers become as American as possible. Scandinavians are sturdy stock: his parents worked around the clock to make ends meet at a hotel they owned near the highway in their town.

When Doug was nineteen, he received a draft notice from the Army. "I wanted to see the world. I figured there'd be a better chance in the Navy." So he enlisted and headed to boot camp where his mom wrote to him every day. He went to sea on the USS *Canberra*. While on station in the Gulf of Tonkin, Doug was blown overboard. Thinking he was dead, his ship held a memorial service for him, but his mother was convinced he was alive. "Everybody thought she was a little crazy. She was mending a pair of my pants, and she set them on her mending stool and she didn't touch them until I came home. Then she said, 'Now you can move them.'"

While his Vietnamese captors were scratching their heads, trying to figure out if his story was true, his fellow prisoners noticed his unusually sharp memory. Dick Stratton says, "When I first met him, he asked me if I knew the Gettysburg Address and we got a rock and wrote it on the floor and he could say it backwards. Now, why you'd want to say it backwards, I don't know, but he could."

Doug reminisces, "I'd always memorized lists of presidents and state capitals, which is kinda trivia. So, why not take that ability and harness it for something practical like memorizing names or camp locations? Eventually, I memorized two hundred and fifty.

"I found that turning the names into a ditty helped. So . . . Lieutenant Colonels Crow, Jim Hughes, James Lamar, Gordon Larson, Robbie Risner, Hervey Stockman, Majors Elmo Baker, Al Brunstrom, Jack Bomar, Dick Bolstad, Don Burns, Ron Byrne, Art Burer, Fred Cherry, Will Cordier, Larry Guarino, James Hiteshaw, Ken Hughey, Sam Johnson, Sam Makowski, Ray Merritt, Al Runyan." He sounds a bit like an auctioneer, running the words together as he effortlessly

spits them out in a single breath. He exhales. "It's always easier to memorize a poem than it is a bunch of meaningless words."

"Even then, I think Commander Stratton thought if they released somebody, they would release me." The senior prisoner in their camp requested he take an early release, for they knew his knowledge would be valuable information. As hard as it was for him to leave behind others who had been held longer, he had been given an order and a mission. For those two hundred and fifty names he memorized gave peace of mind to two hundred and fifty families; they knew their loved one was indeed alive.

Except for his gray hair and a few wrinkles around his small, beady eyes, Doug has retained his boyish looks, shy and humble demeanor, and flat, dry sense of humor. He recently retired after close to thirty years as an instructor at the Navy's POW survival and training school, the first position he took upon returning from Vietnam. A fitting responsiblity for a former POW, the job allowed him to pass on the lessons he learned. "When I retired, they gave me a big shadow box. I got the civilian commendation award. I guess it is one of the highest ones." He shrugs.

He never married or had children. He had a girlfriend for sixteen years, but she died in 1995. He doesn't like to talk about her. He lives by himself in a modest house he owns in Ocean Beach, California, and rides his bike up to six hours every day. "I'm a loner most of the time." He doesn't seem to understand the continued interest in his POW experience.

What's left for him to do? He shrugs. "Well, I was thinking about getting one of those bicycle taxis, you know. Pedal people around and make money. . . . I'd also like to visit Australia. I missed that part of the sea tour on the USS *Canberra* when I fell overboard."

# *Expressions*

## CAPTAIN JAMES L. "DUFFY" HUTTON, USN (RET.)

There was a little mouse that used to come to my cell in the middle of the night. . . . One night, I was lying there around two or three o'clock in the morning. I heard this funny noise coming from the floor and I looked down and saw this mouse. He'd found a piece of sandpaper somewhere and he had it in his mouth and he was also standing on it and the only way he could move was to jump up and drag the piece of sandpaper in his mouth. He went all the way through the cell dragging the piece of sandpaper. . . . So that was my entertainment for the night." And the inspiration for this poem:

**Friends**
Have you ever been locked in a room all alone, for many a month on end?
And never seen a friendly face, a laugh, a smile, a grin?
If you had been locked in a room all alone for many a month on end,
Then you would know how a rat or mouse could become a prisoner's friend.
Now rats and mice make very good friends, they visit you each day.
They're fairly small and quiet and they really like to play.
All my friends were rats or mice, I talked to them each day.
And we did agree that they would not bite, if I would stay out of the way.
I used to feed the rats and the mice that ran around my room.
They helped to keep my spirits high, and chase away the gloom.
So if you are ever locked in a room all alone for many a month on end.
Just look around and you may find, a rat, a mouse, a friend.
                                    —Hanoi, Vietnam 1970

Duffy Hutton has a wry sense of humor and his punch lines are curt. His smile can be devilish. He was nicknamed by his father after a comic strip character that was always getting into trouble. But, he also describes himself as more emotional than most and, indeed, his feelings are much closer to the surface than most men of his generation. He is soft-spoken and reserved, but he gets choked up easily when speaking of his Vietnam experience—or any sad topic, for that matter. He tends to change the subject quickly.

Duffy seems to be able to digest his feelings and express them in a controlled, polished way—by writing poetry. And, indeed, he has an acute aesthetic sense and a well-developed eye for shape and color. His home is tidy and meticulously decorated. But his artistic interests and skills are subtle and he doesn't brag about them. He only talks about them when coaxed. Perhaps they are simply a personal mechanism to manage his emotions?

Duffy first studied poetry as a teenager. "In high school, I had to take a poetry class and I thought it was stupid. But, in prison, the only thing I could remember was Keats's 'Ode to a Grecian Urn.' So, 'Ode to a Porcelain Cup' was a parody."

**Ode to a Porcelain Cup**
Oh, porcelain cup you've served me well, thru these years of waste.
Each time I felt the need of drink, you watered my weathered face.
When we first met many years ago, you were bright and shiny and new.
Now you're dull, chipped and cracked, you've become aged too.
We've been thru a lot together, lo these many years.
Lots of heat, lots of sweat, hours of longing and fear.
But when I leave this forlorn place, as my days in this hell are up.
I'll take along the memory of you, my old porcelain cup.
—Hanoi, Vietnam 1971

When Duffy returned from Vietnam, he finished out his military career as the Executive Officer at the Naval Drug Rehabilitation Center in San Diego. "I got qualified to fly again, but I never did get assigned back to a flight billet. I had lost too much operational experience and my contemporaries were seven years ahead of me." So he retired in 1979 and worked for twenty years as a computer consultant and as a realtor. He and his wife, Eileen, a Navy nurse whom he met at the naval hospital in San Diego shortly after his return from Vietnam, are now fully retired and have one grown son.

His rhymed writing is not a highly practiced talent, but the product of spurts of inspiration that motivate him for short periods of time. "I just sit down and start writing and, in an hour, you know, the poem's written. It's not something I slave over. . . . It just seems to come naturally." Duffy shrugs.

"People ask me what personality trait is the best [to have as a POW] and I'd say having a sense of humor and just not getting too tied up with the fact that, you know, 'I'm here and I can't do anything about it.' You just accept it and hope that someday it will change, which fortunately it did for most of us."

# Tall and Texan

## THE HONORABLE SAMUEL R. JOHNSON,
## U.S. HOUSE OF REPRESENTATIVES AND COLONEL, USAF (RET.)

*I* was born in Texas, I grew up in Texas, and I'm gonna die in Texas." Sam Johnson is tall and lanky and obviously proud of his roots. His presence is imposing, with a set of smoky blue eyes, a hooked nose, and a big, easygoing smile. He quickly lassoes you into his personal space by leaning down, grinning, and eagerly listening. Perhaps that is what made Sam so appealing to his Dallas constituents. He prefers small social and political gatherings, where he can talk to people more intimately. Indeed, he can make you feel like you are the only person in the room. He is gently playful; there is a lot of fun in his voice and in his stories.

As a member of the Thunderbirds, the Air Force's elite flight demonstration team, Sam flew solo for eight months. The selection process for this assignment is fiercely competitive, so "you get to do some things you can't do otherwise. Like, when we went to New York City, I was flying solo at the time and I just decided I'd fly around the Empire State Building. And I did. I turned on the smoke and flew around it." He smiles and takes a defiant bite out of a Hershey bar.

"I graduated from high school when I was sixteen. We used to do it better and quicker and faster in Texas." He pauses for effect. "I was commissioned in the Air Force when I was twenty and I was actually flying at twenty-one [in Korea]." As a fighter pilot in Vietnam, he was shot down on his twenty-fifth mission and spent more than seven years in captivity—forty-two months in solitary confinement, seventy-two days in leg stocks.

But most of Sam's POW experience was shared with Jim Stockdale and Jerry Denton. "When Stockdale and Denton and I were together, we talked a lot about what we'd do [if we got out] and decided that we ought to stop griping about government and see if we couldn't do something about it and get involved. And that's what most of us did, if you recall."

**40**

So, after a distinguished, twenty-nine-year military career, Sam started a home-building business in Dallas and served in the Texas Legislature. Then he ran for Congress in 1991. He didn't find campaigning to be particularly hard. "No, I like meeting people and that's what it's all about. And I think I've found out even here that if you shoot straight with people, they're going to like you and vote for you. They might get mad at you every now and then, but they get over it." And what does he like about Congress? The sheer contrast to his years as a POW. "There's nothin' the same any two days."

As one of few congressmen to have seen combat action—both in Korea and Vietnam—Sam has a biography that gives him a certain license. He is firm in his convictions but also seems somewhat carefree about the political ramifications his actions might have. For Sam has already proven himself. What you see is what you get. He has no agenda other than to represent his district earnestly and honestly and eventually go back to his life in Texas—to Shirley, his wife of fifty-two years, his three children, ten grandchildren, and one great-grandchild.

Texans are a proud people and sometimes a little petulant. "Well, everybody's friendly down there and—I tell you what—you can find anything you want in that state. You know, we talked at one time about joining Oklahoma and Mexico and forming our own state, our own nation. You know Texas can do that? They can secede if they want to. . . . I'm serious." Texans are not shy about telling you how they feel, especially if they're not happy about something. "We just get on our horsey and ride away, ya know?"

# *Sight and Insight*

## FLOYD HAROLD "HAL" KUSHNER, MD, FACS, COLONEL, USA (RET.)

Sitting on a file cabinet next to Hal Kushner's desk is a small print of John Singer Sargent's painting *Gassed*. It portrays a group of World War I soldiers, blinded by mustard gas, bandaged, and lined up to see a medic. "Great painting for an eye doctor, don't ya think?" And poignant for a doctor who had to watch nine of his fellow soldiers die in his arms. As a trained flight surgeon held as a POW in Vietnam for five and a half years, Hal was not permitted to provide the medical attention his fellow captives needed—they died of malnutrition, dysentery, starvation, and untreated wounds resulting from torture. "It would have been so easy for these men to live—[if we'd only had] antibiotics or protein or fluids. I knew what to do but had no means to help them." So many of the POWs held in South Vietnam never made it home. Their stories are less often told.

At the time, "I thought I was just going insane. But it was only brief. It was anger at the enemy, frustration with the situation, and helplessness." But, surprisingly, Hal doesn't "marinate" in the past, as he puts it. "I feel so fortunate to have survived and flourished when so many braver, stronger, and better-trained men did not." He has perspective now and a good life: two grown children, three grandchildren, a devoted girlfriend, and an eighty-four-year-old mother he visits every day.

In his spare time, Hal skis, boats, scuba dives, and plays tennis. Frankly, he doesn't have the time or the interest to tell war stories, although he realizes it is therapeutic for some. He would rather talk about ophthalmology. After selling his private practice, Hal still works as a contract ophthalmologist three days a week. He has served on numerous community boards and has published myriad medical papers. "I like the science of the eye, the discipline—the neurology of the eye. . . . All my patients have serious vision or medical problems related to their eyes. . . . It's never routine."

Hal continues to help, heal, and give the gift of sight. Indeed, he spends a few weeks a year traveling to remote locations all over the world to perform eye surgeries as part of humanitarian medical missions. His volunteer work has taken him to Turkey, Africa, Haiti, India, and Peru. He finds the patients so grateful and the work so fulfilling: he gives individuals a physical window into their world and he gives himself some insight and perspective on his own world.

Hal's other pastime? Reading. "I think books are my life. I read probably three or four books a week. . . . Reading helps me with the present and the future. . . . I read to learn stuff and for pleasure." He reads the Constitution like most would read the Bible and frequently proselytizes on its merits, citing specific passages, and quoting from his favorite American historical political figures: Thomas Jefferson, Theodore Roosevelt, and Robert E. Lee.

Although he was raised Jewish, his true religion was, and still is, the American political system. He grew up in Danville, Virginia—a town located deep in Confederate territory and full of its relics, so his interest in American history was piqued early. He still believes in our system of government as the standard for the world—in all its imperfections—and his faith in the American system is unshakable. Indeed, his experience in Vietnam most likely strengthened it. He swore that, if he was ever released and returned home to the United States, he would learn our country's history in depth. And he did.

"My dad's name was Robert Lee Kushner. My older brother's name was Robert Lee Kushner Jr. And, as you know, Robert E. Lee was commander of the southern forces but a man of great character and a noble soul. He said something that I've always remembered all my life that was taught to me by my father, first said by General Lee. He said, 'Duty is the sublimest word in the language. You can never do more than your duty. You should never wish to do less.'"

# The Guardian

## VICE ADMIRAL WILLIAM P. LAWRENCE, USN (RET.)

*B*red as guard dogs, mastiffs are fiercely territorial. Vetter McCain, name after a notable Marine and a notable U.S. Senator, is no exception. He rarely leaves his master's side—all 240 pounds of him. He is noble, proud, serious, thoughtful, and doggedly defensive of his home—just like his master.

Bill Lawrence is one of those rare individuals who embody legendary strength of mind and body. Throughout his life, he has relied on a combination of acute intellect and a fine-tuned ability to coach his body into action—as a National College Football Hall of Famer, drafter of the U.S. Naval Academy's honor code, renowned Navy test pilot, and survivor of the POW experience. To many colleagues, Bill is larger than life.

This is the man who was the first naval aviator to fly twice the speed of sound in a Navy airplane. He was among the final thirty-two candidates for the Project Mercury program. And he was the senior ranking officer at Camp Vegas, tasked with providing the guidelines and setting the rules for other prisoners in the camp to follow. Ever the guardian of standards—where did he get the strength, the ability, the power?

"I grew up in a family where there was a strong emphasis on both physical and mental activity. I was able to develop a body that could endure all the challenges I had to face in my life." Extreme discipline and challenges—both academically and athletically—motivated Bill. "I loved being a test pilot. It was exciting to determine why an aircraft acted a certain way. I loved analyzing it—it was a tremendous mental challenge." His powerful brain and refined brawn enabled him to excel and survive numerous setbacks: a wife who divorced him and debilitating illnesses that handicapped him physically and sapped him mentally. The stroke he suffered three years ago has lingering physical effects, but his proud, fighting spirit remains intact and has sustained him through these difficult times.

There was a time in Vietnam when he was put in the "hot box"—a dark, unventilated, unlighted cell—for sixty days. To remain sane required focus. Mind over body. So Bill decided to compose a poem in his head. He's a big fan of Sir Walter Scott's ability to create order and rhythm out of words. Perhaps it is no coincidence that Scott was a poet who was also known for his character. Bill especially admires Scott's poem "The Lady of the Lake," a poem formed in masterful iambic pentameter.

"Scott had genius, but I had time. [I said to myself] I'm going to compose a perfect iambic pentameter poem in my head. And I did. When I came back and they

asked me to speak to a joint session of the Tennessee state legislature, I quoted that poem that I had kept in my head all those years." And it became the state poem of Tennessee:

Beauty and hospitality are the hallmarks of Tennessee,
and o'er the world as I may roam
no place exceeds my boyhood home.
And oh how much I long to see
my native land, my Tennessee.

He still seeks out the mental—and physical—challenges. The stroke took away the use of one of his arms, so writing his memoirs and personal correspondence—thoughtful, practiced, and unembellished—is a way for him to maintain both mental and physical discipline. It seems to be a form of therapy. "I'm a big one for waking up and thinking in the middle of the night. I think about all the good ideas and what I want to do the next day." Vetter McCain, the gentle giant whose nighttime breathing is the source of Bill's insomnia, lets out a protective snore.

# A Tree Grows

## LIEUTENANT COLONEL TONY MARSHALL, USAF (RET.)

W hen I'm king, everybody is going to live on a farm. Because then you appreciate the food chain." As a child, Tony Marshall lived on a to bacco farm in Upper Marlboro, Maryland, where he learned to grow vegetables, kill and prepare chickens and pigs for meals, and make dandelion wine. His grandfather, who never finished the fifth grade, was a sharecropper. His mom worked as a housekeeper in "the big house on the hill." The farm's owners were nice, but as an African-American, he knew his place: he was only allowed to enter the owner's house from the back door.

Tony's father was absent for most of his childhood, but his mom, grandfather, and uncles were a steady presence and strong influence. They nurtured him and his younger sister —providing the sustenance, sunshine, and pruning that all seedlings need to grow up strong and confident. His elders were quick to punish him if he acted up or disappointed them. "You know, you do anything to embarrass the family and you're gettin' a beating, no questions asked. . . . Even without a man, you know, my mom was in charge, and there was no doubt about that. She was a parent, she was in charge, and there was no making excuses and no explaining things. It was always, 'Because I said so.' That was always her answer. 'You do it because I said so.'"

Tony's mother, who never finished the sixth grade, was determined he would be educated. "There was no doubt I was going to college. So when the other kids were taken out of school to help with the crops, she told whoever it was in the big house, 'No way, that's not an issue, he's staying in school.'" Tony's mom even convinced one of her employers to help him obtain a congressional appointment to the U.S. Air Force Academy. He was accepted and graduated in 1968, at the height of the Vietnam conflict, one of eight African-Americans in his class. All Tony wanted to do was fly and serve his country. Indeed, his persona is more fighter pilot than African-American. Being black is just another piece of who he is. His family background is just that—a background. He seems to be much more defined and influenced by the discipline and values he received as a child and in the military.

He's not bitter about being shot down or about being a POW for nine months. "You know, I just look at things in perspective and [I think about] who asked me to go over there. I did. I volunteered. So what happened to me was my own fault. There's nobody to blame for it. . . . When you press most of [the POWs,] you

will find that most of us did something wrong, made a mistake, got complacent [in the cockpit]. . . . An awful lot of the time, we were doing something we shouldn't have been doing."

Tony was repatriated with his colleagues in March 1973. He has a collection of his memorabilia—his tin cup, a POW bracelet, a few telegrams sent to his mother—displayed in a glass cabinet in his house next to a host of other mementos he has collected over the years. For him, the POW experience was just part of his Asian tour of duty, along with assignments in Thailand and the Philippines.

And it was in the Philippines that he decided to adopt his housekeeper's four-year-old niece. Although he was single at the time, he adored kids and wanted to pass along the love from his mom, his grandfather, and his uncles. For his daughter, Maria, now twenty-two, it was an opportunity for an education and a much better life. "I was the first unmarried male to adopt a female child in the Philippines." The only question the judge had for him? "Who's going to fix her hair?" He lied and said that his sister would make sure her hair was presentable.

He finished out his career in the Air Force, retiring as a lieutenant colonel in 1990, and now flies for United Airlines. He also substitute teaches in the local school district and plans to teach full time when he retires from flying. He lives on a full acre of land with his wife of ten years, Veta, in the California high desert town of Apple Valley. Tony sits comfortably in his backyard, surveying his piece of terra firma. His perpetually relaxed stance and his soulful eyes belie a tough inner core. His family has come a long way in three generations, and he is the fruit of their efforts.

"I love it. An acre is just perfect. . . . I have my purple locust and this is a honey locust and there's a black locust down the rest of the way. . . . I've got fruitless plums and flowering plums. And then there are little peach trees along the fence over there and a couple of apples and walnuts stuck in there. I just love trees."

# The Connoisseur

## VICE ADMIRAL EDWARD H. MARTIN, USN (RET.)

*T*his is one of my favorite appetizers. In the sauce pan is cracked pepper, a little salt, and freshly ground nutmeg." He grinds it by hand in a nutmeg grinder.

"Next, I add butter and let it dissolve and melt in there." Ed Martin is a serious cook, a true gastronome. "Now, I crack the eggs, one at a time. They must be at room temperature. . . . Making *gougres*—pronounced goo-zhair—is a little touchy, so you must stay right with them every moment. You can only use a wooden spoon—it won't work with a metal one." He mixes the dough until it is the texture of silk. "This is how you want it. Smooth and silky. They are rolled into little dough balls and baked for ten to fifteen minutes until they're golden brown and good lookin'!" He likes to eat them hot, washed down liberally with fine champagne.

Ed is a proud and colorful man—with dancing blue eyes, a plume-like posture, and a cadence in his voice that is both lilting and commanding. He preens when showing his home and exquisite collections. His garden is replete with roses, bougainvillea, kona coffee tree plants, snow bushes, plumeria, fuchsia, geraniums, and peppers. Ah yes, the peppers. Bright orange habanero peppers that he uses to concoct his notorious, fiery pepper juice that marinates in the refrigerator for more than three months before being served. It gives his favorite foods that extra punch. Everyone knows they're in for a culinary treat when they come to the Martins' house.

Ed is juicy—he practically salivates just talking about his favorite things. He is proud of his accomplishments and finds the fun in everything he does. Perhaps his prison experience is just what fueled this passion for the finer things in life: good food, exotic travel, and fine furniture. He also doesn't mind talking about his experience in Vietnam or his distinguished Navy career. He is fre-

52

quently asked by local and national media to comment on events in the Middle East and issues involving terrorism, naval strategy, and Vietnam.

Even after spending nearly six years as a prisoner in North Vietnam, "I felt so strongly about our being in Vietnam that I would have volunteered to go back. Not many people would say that." He's right. This type of dedication is not born of blind faith, but rather a rare type of loyalty and optimism. Surprisingly, Ed says he never lost faith in his government. "I never got despondent. I was determined to defeat them." He always expected to return to his home, his family, his career, and his happiness.

And his wife, Sherry, kept this hope alive back home. Sherry has provided the unwavering support, encouragement, and total devotion that has propelled his career and fed his self-confidence. It's a traditional marriage—a solid, enduring one. She sustains him.

Ed has no regrets. "I contributed to the defense of our country in a particularly contentious time and continued to do so long after our release from North Vietnam. I'm an energetic, dynamic person who cares about people. I think those qualities, coupled with dedication and solid leadership skills, are what enabled me to make Admiral."

Ed washes each dish immediately after using it. Not a simple task, given the complexity of his recipes and the detailed attention he pays to each ingredient. "I'm a clean-the-kitchen cook. I don't like clutter." What's his favorite thing to cook? He flashes his famously heartfelt grin and rubs his belly. "Everything!"

# *Golden*

## The Honorable John S. McCain, U.S. Senator and Captain, USN (Ret.), and the Honorable Orson G. Swindle III

O rson!" John McCain's face contorts and he barks out of the corner of his mouth a guttural rendition of his best friend's name, reminiscent of Wallace Berry or a Marine gunnery sergeant but with obvious endearing qualities. They greet each other with bear hugs and testosterone-filled chuckles. They have seen each other at their worst and at their best.

Best friends since their days as prison roommates in Vietnam, John and Orson know each other better than most spouses do. They make an odd pair: Orson is tall and imposing and 100 percent Marine, while John is much shorter, wiry, and full of pluck. They love to tease each other. They tapped on the walls in between their prison cells for months before they even met. In one of their first conversations, John told Orson how he had wanted so much to be a Marine but was disqualified because his parents were married. Orson got back at him. He would tantalizingly describe prison yard scenes that were conveniently out of John's view. "Let me see! Let me see!" was John's childlike plea to Orson.

Never one to mince words, Orson still tells John exactly like it is. "With Orson, everything in life is black and white. It's right and it's wrong. There's good and there's evil. That's a wonderful way to be. In this nuance town in which we live, it's nice to be around somebody who will differentiate between the proper and the improper, the right and wrong, the good and evil."

What do they have in common? The aviator's wings of gold that were pinned on their chests some four decades ago. But, more importantly, they have shared experiences in wartime and peacetime that have drawn them together time and time again: combat, being prisoners of war, and politics. They don't always agree, but they believe in the other's commitments. There is an intrinsic trust that lets them relax and exhale around each other.

"I am very proud of what John has done. He has always responded to me when I called, when I offered criticism, and we have this mutual admiration and respect that essentially does not question our motives because we trust each other and know that the motives are always well-intended."

In the Washington world of casual and superficial acquaintances where debts are social and handshakes are ephemeral—they last as long as the photographer needs to take the official photo—Orson and John have a friendship that demands no favors, holds no grudges, and has been forged in blood—literally.

John says, "My friends are the ones that I served with in the military, with rare exceptions. . . . Those who have illusions about the great friends you can make around [Washington] find out, much to their dismay, [that] amnesia is a severe affliction around this town when you're out of office." True friendships are malleable: they can be tested and even abused, but they rarely lose their luster. They're good as gold.

# Perspective

## Captain John Michael McGrath, USN (Ret.)

roportion is the hardest part for me." Stepping back from his work and tilting his head, Mike McGrath surveys some of his early drawings and paintings. "My style of artwork changed as a result of my experience in Vietnam. Before, it was loose. When I came back, I was more intense. I tried to be more accurate and realistic."

The years since Vietnam have been good to Mike. A retired naval aviator and retired United Airlines pilot, he has been married to Marlene for forty years, and they are five-time grandparents. He lives comfortably in Colorado Springs and exercises at the U.S. Air Force Academy gym every morning at 0515.

His house is filled with his own drawings and paintings and other artwork he and Marlene have collected along the way. What inspires him? "I like good contrasts and depths." When moved to draw, he will frequently use scrap paper or napkins as a medium, a habit he picked up in Vietnam. "You'd be amazed at how your ingenuity really comes through in a time like that."

Mike's creative streak was encouraged at an early age, when he would watch his father paint. "I still remember my father mixing colors and shading a drawing of Bambi when I was about four or five years old." Encouraged by his mother, he took up drawing himself and has refined his craft over the years, always self-taught.

"I'm not a passionate artist. I am more structured, like an architect. I once wanted to study architecture but went to the Naval Academy instead. I liked the tightness, the structure of architectural renderings. It fascinated me. I liked their use of ink and watercolor—mixed media. I still use that technique."

Hoping to document his prison time when he returned home from Hanoi, he picked up pen and paper and began furiously sketching. "I thought about all the subjects I wanted to do for six years. The summer I returned, I took my family on a long camping trip to rebuild our relationship. My drawing effort became quite intense as I tried to catch up and capture the images I had kept in my mind. The result was about sixty drawings that were intended for my family but were later published in a book." *Prisoner of War: Six Years in Hanoi* is in its tenth printing after twenty-seven years in print.

Mike has also used his creative talent for his friends and family. "I made gifts for my fellow prisoners. I made a little cross out of a dog bone for my wife. I whittled it on a chunk of concrete and shined it with a cloth, then drilled a hole

in the top with a wire. It took hundreds of hours to make. I sewed it into the crotch of my underwear so the guards wouldn't confiscate it. I was able to hide it for two years. My wife now keeps it in a safety deposit box at the bank."

The artistic pieces he has made over the years for his fellow prisoners are some of their most treasured possessions. "I did a drawing for Ross Terry and he had it hanging up behind his bar. One day, his house was burning down—it burned to the ground. He ran in and he only had time to grab one thing and he grabbed that drawing I did for him from behind the bar and ran out of the house."

His quickly and intricately composed drawings of captivity and torture are his legacy. They elicit strong emotions from observers. Starkly etched, the pen-and-ink sketches are simple in their rendering, but Mike's bustling, peripatetic energy emerges through the pulsating pen strokes. Any viewer will immediately recognize the complexity of the artist behind the work.

Mike seems nonplused by the reactions his art evokes, but he is proud none-theless. He knows his work will outlive him. He shrugs and chuckles, "I would have liked the twists of the ropes to be even tighter and more realistic, but I couldn't find a willing model."

# The Apostle

## MAJOR GENERAL EDWARD J. MECHENBIER, USAF

A s a native son of Dayton, Ohio, Ed Mechenbier learned about aviation early in life. As the cradle of the industry, his midwestern home served as a breeding ground for his fascination with planes. He attended air show open houses at nearby Wright-Patterson Air Force Base as a child. But it wasn't until he was on his way to the U.S. Air Force Academy that he got his first taste. "The very first time I was ever on an airplane was on the 26th of June, 1960, when I got onto a TWA SuperG Constellation." And he found religion.

"I loved the Air Force Academy. I relished the challenge and I enjoyed the place. I was not a genius—had a 2.83 GPA, but I did well militarily. . . . It goes back to why I'm still doing this. It's not just the flying, but because I like the whole environment." Ed speaks at a faster clip now. His enthusiasm envelops you. "I'm going to get a little hokey with you, but there is really something to this integrity, service, and excellence we have—our core values in the Air Force. They mean something; they weren't just created a few years ago; they epitomize what the Air Force is all about. So, if you fly airplanes or if you buy airplanes, design airplanes, or if you're out working at a depot somewhere, or if you're a lawyer or a doctor and you're in this Air Force, you're part of one of the really neatest teams and entities in all the world. And I firmly and passionately believe this. . . . You don't have to have one of these," referring to the stars on his shoulders.

Ed's active schedule seems to preserve his youthful presence. Tall, lean, and jocular, he has an energy level of someone half his age. He holds down both an executive job with defense contractor SAIC and an Air Force Reserve position. He is still qualified to fly a number of aircraft and he provides the live commentary at the Miramar Air Show in San Diego every year. The cadence of his voice and the acuity of his perceptions make him a natural for the job.

Ed always seems to be one step ahead and he makes it seem easy. As a two-star general stationed at the same Wright-Patterson Air Force Base where he meandered as a kid, Ed is one of the last Vietnam-era POWs still wearing a uniform. He simply doesn't want to retire. Why not? "I'm still flying . . . that's a motivator. I have more than enough years to retire, but I have no intention of retiring. Where else can you do what we're doing? *And I still get to fly*. That's icing on a good cake, right there."

Happy-go-lucky with a dry wit, Ed doesn't dwell on much—especially not

the past. He figures he was within two seconds of dying when he ejected from his burning aircraft in Vietnam. But he still wakes up every morning pinching himself that he is still here and has all his arms and legs. As he describes it, "Being happy doesn't mean everything in the world is wonderful; it means you've just learned to look beyond the imperfections."

Ed and his wife have four children, three adopted—one of whom is Vietnamese-American. The irony doesn't seem to register with him. "We adopted a child who happened to be Vietnamese. The priest in Fairborn, Ohio, had a sister who was a Charity nun and ran an orphanage in South Vietnam." The baby girl was found in a shoebox in a ditch outside the orphanage. "So, that's how we got Mahli." According to him, Mahli never considered herself Asian until she applied to college and realized she had three advantages over other applicants: she is a woman, a minority, and a war orphan. "She was raised American and never really asked about her birth parents." She is now a twenty-seven-year-old prosecuting attorney in Stark County, Ohio, and is married to a Danish-American doctor with Polish-Danish parents. Only in America.

"Obviously, from my experience, people ask me if I have any animosity towards her [or the Vietnamese]. Those people were doing what they were taught to do. They were told they were fighting the bad, evil Americans and we were fighting the bad, evil Vietnamese." He shrugs his shoulders. "We were praying to the same God." Pause. "Hey, wanna go to lunch? My favorite restaurant is a Vietnamese restaurant about three hundred yards from here." He adjusts his military cover and jumps out the door.

# The Professor

## Captain Ernest M. "Mel" Moore Jr., USN (Ret.)

*H*e catalogs his collections by geographic origin—country or continent. Methodically, deliberately, and almost fervently, Mel Moore researches new collectibles—cameos, Chinese snuff bottles, mabe pearls, Asian porcelain, or antique marbles. "I get interested in one particular thing and pursue it to the ultimate and then, the next week, I'm into something else. It keeps me out of trouble." Mel can wax authoritatively, albeit somewhat esoterically, about the origins of his ceramics and keeps abreast with his board activity at the San Francisco Ceramics Circle, which meets monthly at the Palace of the Legion of Honor.

He acquires his treasures and artfully displays the pieces around his simple fishing cabin on Bethel Island in the Delta region of the San Francisco Bay. A native of northern California, Mel takes comfort in the familiar surroundings of this remote town, a place he spent summers as a youth with his high school friend's family, fishing and "chasing girls."

"I found this place and love it 'cause I can be isolated, but if I want to go someplace, I can go a reasonable distance. . . . Being independent and reclusive is not one of my . . . well, I don't have any problems entertaining myself." Is he reclusive? "Some people would consider [me so,] but I don't think so at all. But I tend to mind my own business, let me put it that way." Is he a hermit? "Not at all. There are too many things I enjoy going out and doing."

"Most of my time [in captivity] was isolated—twenty-two months solitary confinement, sixteen months straight—or with one or a few men . . . longer than most, but not as long as some." And, yet, Mel now seems to relish his self-imposed solitude. He retreated to this peaceful and rustic spot twelve years ago. He lives alone and keeps himself occupied researching, acquiring, and cataloging his collections.

Did his penchant for academic and solitary pursuits help him survive the extreme isolation, or did his extended time "in jail" form habits that are hard to break? He thinks the fact that he is quite content by himself did help him better cope with the extended periods of solitary confinement in Hanoi. "I have always been a loner." In contrast, he said there were men who succumbed to the conditions and just died. What makes him different? His ingenuity.

Educated at the University of California at Berkeley, the University of San Francisco, the Naval Postgraduate School, USIU, and National University, Mel is a natural intellectual and studies problems like he studies his collections—

turning them over, looking at them from all sides. While in captivity at the Hanoi Hilton, he could hear Ben Pollard in a nearby cell crying out in pain from severe injuries and calling for his wife, Joan. He was black from his waist to his knees from internal bleeding and, according to Mel, "was out of his head ranting." Mel looked at the situation practically and intellectually. He figured his captors had a severe problem on their hands: a hallucinating man. So he took a chance and asked an interrogator if he could be put in a cell with Ben to help him. This type of request was unprecedented, but it was granted. Mel had the solution. As Ben recounts, "Mel started to take care of me. He said, 'You walk or you die.' There was no doubt about it. He saved my life."

Brilliant in his knowledge of history and art, and professorial in his pursuit of antiques and collectibles, Mel is surprisingly unreflective about his personal life, other than to lament that he doesn't understand why he and his wife, Chloe, divorced after twenty-nine years of marriage. Nonetheless, when asked who his best friend is, without missing a beat, he says, "Chloe."

While many fighter pilots are known for their social excesses, Mel channels this proclivity toward his collections. He has been sober for fifteen years and displays his Alcoholics Anonymous pin prominently, along with his distinguished naval service mementos. He says he loves life and doesn't miss drinking at all. In fact, he says he enjoys social gatherings more since he has been sober.

He tempers his philosophical outlook with a strong dose of reality. He is politically conservative, but this is tempered by personal testaments to the horrors of war. "Once you've been involved in killing someone . . . and you know it . . . it makes you come to grips with reality. I tend to be a philosopher and interested in . . . what causes us to fight each other." Ever didactic, he pauses for effect. "People don't understand how grim war really is."

# *Divine Intervention*

## CAPTAIN RICHARD D. "MOON" MULLEN, USN (RET.), AND MRS. PEGGY MULLEN

S he winked at me and gave me permission to get on with my life."
There in the midst of a chilly December sunset, Dick Mullen was taking a walk along the beach near his La Jolla home on his deceased wife's birthday. As he watched the sun slowly melt into the Pacific Ocean, Dick saw the elusive green flash. "I know some people don't believe you can actually see it, but I saw it that night and, in that instant, I realized that Jean wanted me get out of my doldrums and move on."

He said he needed a jolt, something to motivate him to do more than "tread water." Seeing the brief, evergreen spark of light warmed and energized him. He became active again in his church and the local Kiwanis club. Then he met Peggy, a recent widow, who enjoyed biking and tennis and shared his strong faith. Dick describes her entry into his life as divine intervention.

For those who are blessed with a long-term, happy marriage, the loss of a spouse is most devastating. For Dick, the grief was almost more than he could bear. He was married to his first wife for more than forty years, a match he called "as close to perfect as a marriage could be." Their union even survived six years of separation when he was a POW. Then, she came down with cancer and died. He slipped into a despondent state that worried his friends.

Dick and Peggy met through mutual friends at church and the coincidences in their life were uncanny. They married six months later and the couple has been blissful. As long time La Jolla residents, they are well recognized in the community as the pair who cycles through La Jolla on their tandem bike, a wedding gift from Dick's children.

"Life is wonderful." Some might find it difficult to understand how Dick has such a positive outlook after six years in prison in North Vietnam and the loss of his beloved wife to cancer. He is amazingly calm, gentle-natured, and at peace with himself and his place in life. Does he ever get mad or feel bitter?

"No. I have always felt God's presence. . . .When I climbed up on my bed, another POW had scratched on the wall of the cell, 'God, Country, Family'—in small letters. It was an old, old whitewashed cell that was sort of dirty after all those years and, when you scratch on the whitewash, the white will really show through—just in small letters. When I started thinking about God being ever present and His infinite love, I just opened my mind to His ever-presence. In this hopeless situation, that's indeed the sensation and feelings I got. It was much like when you're trying to write a book and the words aren't coming at first. And then, pretty soon, your story just starts to flow and really starts to open up. . . . So I knew that He was with me."

# *Soaring*

## Colonel Ben M. Pollard, USAF (Ret.)

*L*ift (lift) n. 5. the upward pressure air exerts on an aircraft in flight. 6. A feeling of elation." (Oxford American Dictionary)
"It really is kind of like breathing. Once you do it, I don't know why, but it just makes sense." To fly in a glider, you just have to find the lift. "Birds do the same thing we do. So if you see a hawk or an eagle soaring in a circle, hey, you go right over there, and sure enough you'll find out that there's lift. One day when I was flying, I looked up and saw this eagle and I went up and got on the lift he was in. We were going up right with him. Oh, it was spectacular!"

Ben Pollard started gliding when he was the deputy commander for military instruction at the U.S. Air Force Academy after his return from Vietnam. He supervised much of the cadets' training, including their formal military instruction, navigation, parachuting, and flying. While he was always enamored of jets, he found the quiet solitude of a glider to be intoxicating. So he became an instructor and has been doing it ever since. Now that he has been medically grounded from flying jets, soaring keeps him connected to aviation—one of his primary, lifelong loves.

His other love? Joan, his wife of forty-eight years. "My wife did a superb job of raising these kids while I was gone and it's really showing." Both his son and daughter are engineers—just like Ben, so Joan obviously kept the memories of their father fresh during the six years he was in captivity. For the first three and a half years he was gone, he was listed as missing. Joan didn't know whether he was alive or dead: was she a wife or a widow?

When Ben was shot down, he broke his back and suffered severe internal bleeding—he was paralyzed from the waist down. The torture he was subjected to only exacerbated his injuries. He was alive, but barely holding on, and he was wildly hallucinating from the pain, crying out for Joan. He credits Mel Moore with saving him. "Mel heard me screaming. . . . He talked an officer into letting him come into my cell. Never happened before—that I know of. He came in, found me naked, lying in my excretion, as near death as you can be. And he began to help me. . . . I said, 'Oh Mel, I hurt so much.' He says, 'Listen, you walk or you die. You walk or you die.'" So Ben walked. Together, it took six months of daily therapy. And he and Mel are still best friends.

Retired from both the Air Force and a stint as vice president of a long distance phone company, Ben still suffers from his injuries and endures a lot of

daily pain. He also has undergone seven bypasses, had two major heart attacks, arthritis, and a bout with colitis that has left him without his lower intestine. So, he enjoys every day of retirement.

There's an easiness about Ben that is relaxing. His mannerisms are graceful. His tall and lanky figure is more protective than towering; he is earnest, gentle, and centered on his surroundings—not himself. His focus is on soaking in the every day, buoyed by the small pleasures: going to the theater, seeing his children raise grandchildren, and growing beautiful succulents in his desert garden in Poway, California. For he knows firsthand the power of positive thinking, and he refuses to dwell in the "tragedy of self-pity," as he terms it. No, he feels lucky. "Hell, I'm alive. I've gotten thirty years that friends of mine didn't get."

The amount of lift determines the length of the flight.

# Taming a Legend

## Brigadier General Robinson Risner, USAF (Ret.), and Mrs. Dorothy Risner

Horses were my first love. I had a kindredship with them. Back in Oklahoma, adults used to hire me to go out and catch them. I would pretend to be playing with something in the grass and [the horses] would get curious." Then came World War II and fighter jets. Robbie Risner couldn't wait to join up. "With rodeo horses, I liked finding out about their dispositions. With jets, I liked finding out about their attributes and how to get the maximum performance out of them. I trained myself at their expense. I ate and slept fighters. They responded so wonderfully."

Robbie was a notorious fighter pilot in Korea. The twentieth American jet "ace," he shot down eight enemy aircraft. He broke the transatlantic speed record set by Charles Lindbergh. His air-to-air combat stories shock even the most seasoned pilots. He survived two shoot downs in Vietnam and seven years' torturous captivity in Hanoi, only to come home and face colossal personal challenges. He and his first wife divorced and she later died of lung cancer. His son died of a congenital heart defect. He has been twice diagnosed with cancer and his current wife, Dot, has also suffered from cancer. The legendary fighter pilot found himself dodging bullets on the home front left and right. "Experience and God helped me get through those things. [When] I was in solitary confinement for four years, the only person I had to talk to was God—I kept the line pretty hot! . . . [So,] I had a firm grip on things when I returned, and I thought, What can they do to hurt me? Emotionally, I was pretty stable."

What gave him this unshakable conviction? As the senior Air Force officer in the Hanoi prison system, how did he maintain unity, organization, and morale within a temperamental and restless group of men who could only communicate by tapping on walls? "It was a peculiar leadership style because you had very little eye-to-eye contact. It was all done by remote, covert communications." He

72

had to make an impact with his words—or taps—and the looming presence of his almost mythical reputation. "The first sign of a good leader is consideration of the men under you. . . . If you consider others first in whatever you're striving for, when others know that you are sincerely interested in their welfare, they in turn will support you." It was that simple to him.

Robbie seems completely at peace with himself and his life. He counts his wife of twenty-five years as the greatest blessing of his life. He and Dot are retired in San Antonio and take great pleasure in their fourteen grandchildren.

Robbie's physical presence is suffused with softness: sad eyes, gentle voice, delicate touch. He doesn't have the traditional chiseled features most fighter pilots sport but those of a man who has learned and been humbled by his life's experiences.

He credits his faith with smoothing out the rough edges and taming his wild streak. "It's kind of like having a bunch of dice in a box. You shake 'em around long enough and it wears the corners off and they become marbles. Human life is a little like that. You expose them to different personalities, different wants and desires and needs, and it doesn't leave you with too many rough edges. That's what I've found."

# Relative Motion

## Major Wesley D. Schierman, USAF (Ret.)

*E*ach morning they would send a car down to pick me up and they'd drive me up the hill to the base hospital. It was a thirty miles-per-hour speed limit and when this driver would go up the hill at thirty, it felt to me like it was about seventy. It was like the telephone poles, everything, were moving like this." Wes Schierman whips his arms across his face. "I hadn't seen relative motion for so long, you know, nothing that moved that fast and I really didn't know: was that going to carry over into my flying? . . . It was just startling to think about how messed up my senses were." After almost seven and a half years in captivity, Wes was in the middle of his physical debriefing at Travis Air Force Base, and he feared he wouldn't be able to get back in the cockpit.

Two weeks later, back home in Spokane, Washington, his old National Guard unit gave him a back seat ride in a T-33 training jet. It was much slower than the F-105 he had flown eight years before, but he hoped it would help him to get his feet wet again. He was nervous. "But I did find that I could get the airplane around fairly well on instruments. . . . On landing, I got the gear and flaps down and started to turn final. Unconsciously, the air speed seemed so low that I felt like I was going to fall out of the sky. I kept pushing the power up and the guy in front would be pulling it back, saying, 'You're too hot, slow down.' It was quite amazing; I was still carrying the sensations of the last thing I had flown, the F-505." And his confidence was coming back.

Flying is the only thing Wes has ever wanted to do professionally. Growing up on a farm in eastern Washington, Wes said he hated "chugging along on the tractor." He used to look up longingly at the planes passing overhead. Forty years later, Wes is now in the midst of his third aviation career. After flying for the Air Force and the Air National Guard for fifteen and a half years (twenty-one

75

years in the Reserves) and then piloting Northwest Airlines jets for twenty-three years, he is now flying experimental airplanes. At first, he wasn't interested in these "kit" planes. Wes likes to fly fast and drive fast. "I'm always in a hurry. Too many things to do, the clock is ticking. I've gotta keep moving." So, these planes didn't seem speedy enough or big enough for his taste.

"But, this friend of mine who was also a Northwest pilot was raving about how cool it was, how neat, how fun it was. . . . I finally agreed to go for a ride with him and I thought, 'Boy, this is fun, it's just like a little fighter.' One thing

led to another and I ended up buying one. . . . We've now worked our way up from two of us to twenty-eight of us, over about thirteen years." He and the squadron they call the Blackjacks conduct flight demonstrations in close formation at air shows, Memorial Day events, and weddings. He's having a ball.

The precision and discipline required to fly planes is the most rewarding and challenging part to Wes. The satisfaction of continually striving to fly in perfect formation or make a perfect landing is what he enjoys the most. "I've been flying for more than forty years. I'm far more experienced now, and I know when I can push the envelope with these little planes." He smiles an impish grin, "Of course, it's easier when no one is shooting at you."

Unlike many of his POW colleagues, Wes admits that he does harbor some bitterness from his Vietnam experience. His anger is more directed toward those who were his country's political leaders at the time; the more he reads about his government's actions during the war, the more disillusioned he becomes. He just can't dwell on it. "One of the main things I've concluded over the years is, as human beings, we tend to forget the bad and remember the good. And the first thing I think about [the POW experience] is the great people I had a chance to serve with. . . . They're all great Americans, great patriots, great role models and they amaze me. They're like something that I thought was only in books."

Is it speed that helps Wes cope? Or is it the fact that flying enables him to continue to move forward, even if it's only relative? In all actuality, Wes's activities help him continually look forward and keep the past in the past and the bad experiences in the back of his mind—just where he wants them. He lets them slip by, just like those telephone poles. As his granddaughter, Cassie, says to him, "What's the next fun thing we're going to do, Grandpa?"

# The Nor'easter

## Captain Edwin A. Shuman III, USN (Ret.)

N ed Shuman watches the Weather Channel because everything he likes to do depends on the weather: sailing, flying, hunting. His sailboat is conveniently berthed in the backyard of his Nantucket-style house—right on Weems Creek in Annapolis, Maryland. Every summer, he sails the boat up to the Newport, Rhode Island, harbor and lives onboard. His wife, Dona, comes up on weekends.

Ned first started sailing when he was about five, growing up in Marblehead, Massachusetts. "My dad was a yacht broker before World War II and quite a sailor and yacht designer. He got us into it early." Ned dropped out of Michigan State and joined the Navy at seventeen because his dad had liked the sea service so much. "He kinda talked me into it. Then, once I got in, he said, 'Why don't you go to the Naval Academy?' I said they would never take me." But they did. Ned graduated in 1954 and became a pilot. His father only recently died at age ninety-three. He has a picture of "the old man," as he calls him, in his front hall.

You can tell Ned was raised on the New England coast: he still has a hint of a Massachusetts accent and he is sharp-tongued and feisty, his crusty personality punctuated by his steely blue eyes and sun-weathered skin. His friends jokingly call him Nasty Ned. Facetiously, he says, "I can't even fathom why some misinformed individuals call me that." But Ned's bluster also has a genteel quality to it. He looks comfortable in yachting attire, sitting at the helm of a large sailboat, charming his guests with his wickedly flirtatious wit. You can picture him in his heyday, holding court at the officer's club.

Ned's Vietnam experience was hard on his family, and his return home was not an easy adjustment. The first thing he did was to buy a boat. "I packed my three kids, who hadn't seen me in five years, and my [first] wife who hadn't seen me in five years—and we went on a three-month cruise." He learned a lot from that trip, perhaps more than he did as a POW. "It was horrible. We ended up getting divorced, and it was pretty miserable on the kids." In retrospect, he says, he probably should have put more of his children's needs ahead of his own. He also stopped drinking and he has been sober for more than twenty years.

After serving as a squadron commander at the Naval Air Station Oceana and working at the Naval Safety Center, Ned ran the Naval Academy's sailing program. He spent his final tour in the Navy as the officer in charge of the Naval Annex in Bermuda, a fitting assignment for a yachtsman. Now fully retired, he continues to compete in the biannual Newport–Bermuda race.

Ned likes retirement, as he doesn't really have to adhere to any particular schedule. With his own sailboat and his own airplane, he can go where he wants when he wants. He is more reflective now and seems to recognize, albeit reluctantly, how his personality has mellowed over the years. He is less stormy. But he's not sure if it's because of age or being sober or the POW experience. "I'm not as ambitious as I used to be. I hope I'm not as selfish. I think I treat people a little better now. . . . And I'm a much better grandfather than I was a father. I'd like to think the POW experience has made me a better person, but [sometimes] I don't think it has. . . . I used to say, 'If I ever get out of this goddamn place, nothing will ever bother me again.' [Now,] I'll go upstairs and pull three socks out of the bureau drawer and two of them won't match and I'll kick 'em all the way across the room. . . . So, maybe you just don't change." He shrugs and smiles a little more softly.

# The Music Man

## Captain C. Everett Southwick, USN (Ret.)

Every man in his generation served, but only a select few served in the Navy's elite pilot community. The aviators are always easy to spot and Ev Southwick is no exception. He's a man's man with ruddy good looks—an eagle's posture, a wide-stepped saunter, flirtatious brown eyes that sparkle in the company of women, weathered hands that grip you like a vise, and a distinctly baritone voice. With Ev, however, you also can't mistake the music in his laugh.

As a loyal Husky, "I started singing in 1949 at the University of Washington. A fraternity brother told me to walk down to University Avenue and buy a 'Hawaiian O' C.F. Martin ukulele. I paid $18.75—now it's worth more than $800! We played and sang all over sorority row. One of my favorites was, and still is, 'Be Prepared.'" Good advice for an aviator. "I still bring the ukulele out on occasion at parties—when the spirit moves me."

"Be prepared! That's the Boy Scouts' marching song/Be prepared! As through life you march along/Be prepared to hold your liquor pretty well/Don't write naughty words on walls if you can't spell." — Tom Lehrer

In Navy flight training, Ev sang in the Naval Aviation Cadet Choir. "In October 1953, we traveled to New York to appear on the Ed Sullivan Show. The camera slowly panned the choir, so each of us had about 1.5 seconds of fame." Ev immediately breaks into laughter, a deep-bellied roar normally reserved for Saint Nick.

Ev was shot down near Than Hoa in May 1967 and spent just shy of six years in the infamous Hanoi Hilton. To entertain their fellow prisoners, he and a few of his friends formed a singing group. "I was part of a quartet in Vietnam. We also had our own choir, and I was involved in church services there."

Good singing comes from deep within and the music in Ev's life is a distinct window into his soul. A high-spirited individual with a perpetually sunny outlook, Ev's playful nature and sense of humor are his own personal therapy in action. It has sustained him through painful times in his life, including a brain aneurysm and three divorces.

He doesn't describe himself as particularly religious in a formal sense; rather, singing and laughter seem to serve as his spiritual release. "People often shake their heads and comment to me that they could never have survived what I have. You know what? They're wrong. The human spirit has amazing fortitude and, faced with such a challenge, can muster incredible strength. Common men have proven this time and time again."

# *The Thespian*

## VICE ADMIRAL JAMES BOND STOCKDALE, USN (RET.), AND MRS. SYBIL STOCKDALE

*I*t was a dramatic ploy and a desperate one. Exasperated with the status quo in Hanoi and his inability to effect change within the prison system that had incarcerated and tortured him and his colleagues for years, Jim Stockdale knew he had to do something. When he was told he was going "downtown," he knew what it meant. He was going to be cleaned up and paraded in front of anti-war activists or sympathetic journalists to counter Western allegations that the American POWs were being treated inhumanely.

Jim refused to be a pawn. So he staged a fake suicide attempt. Uncertain of the impact and ramifications his actions would have, he just followed his instincts. Breaking a cell window, he took the glass shards and repeatedly cut his wrists. Then, he beat himself with a wooden plank to a bloody, bruised pulp. With his piercing blue eyes, he appeared half-dead and half-crazy. For the first time, his Vietnamese captors were scared of him. These actions effectively changed the entire prison dynamic. Nothing was ever the same again: prison conditions improved and the torture sessions ceased . . . for good. As Jim described it, "I'd been looking for the keys to the kingdom for seven years, and I'd found 'em."

To what does he ascribe his ability to trick the system? "I'm an actor! I've been acting since I was a kid." An actor? "I had the lead in every high school play, and Mom knew most of those plays well," he declares in the book *In Love and War*. "We would talk about my interpretation of the parts at home. In my last play, my senior year, we began arguing about the male lead's part. From the way I described my feelings about it, she was convinced I was way off track, that I was creating a character quite different from the one she would have her actor portray. I was confident I knew what I was doing." With an early stage presence and an innate instinct for the lead character's influence on the drama, he used the art of acting as a tool. His mother imparted this inner power and strength to him.

Sybil, his wife of fifty-five years, took over that coaching role.

Was Jim Stockdale chosen for the lead in Vietnam or did he choose it himself? Schooled in the doctrine of Epictetus at Stanford University prior to going to Vietnam, Jim was a follower of the Stoics and credits the philosophy with providing him his moral sustenance and direction. But he wrote the script. And it earned him the Medal of Honor.

> Remember that you are an actor in a drama of such sort as the author chooses—if short, then in a short one: if long, then in a long one. If it be his pleasure that you should enact a poor man, see that you act it well; or a cripple, or a ruler, or a private citizen. For this is your business—to act well the given part; but to choose it belongs to Another. — Enchiridion 17, Epictetus

# *Listening*

## CAPTAIN RICHARD A. STRATTON, USN (RET.),
### AND GRANDDAUGHTERS ALLYSON, ASHLEY, AND AMANDA

*W*hat do you want? Do you want juice or do you want milk? . . . I'll give you some juice. Can you say please? Thank you." Dick Stratton exudes calm and patience and seems to enjoy the twirls and high-pitched antics of three little girls underfoot. For this is his "A" team of granddaughters: Ashley, Amanda, and Allyson. Providing a willing ear and good advice is a skill Dick has well steeped.

Perhaps he absorbed it from his parents as a young Irish Catholic kid in Quincy, Massachusetts. His mother, Mary, was a secretary by day but more often found herself in the role of the community therapist. "My mom was the neighborhood counselor. Everyone came by to talk to her—to lay it on her. . . . She was approachable, nonjudgmental, maintained confidentiality, humble, and an all-around nice person. She would not tolerate gossip or slander or negativity about anyone or any group." And his father? "You become a good listener when you recognize the wisdom of my father who always said, 'You never learn anything when you're talking.'"

Perhaps he learned to listen at Catholic seminary where he spent six years in prayerful meditation and observation. He left right before he was to be ordained and, instead, pursued a degree at Georgetown University and a commission in the Navy. When it came right down to it, he said, he just didn't have the calling. "I wanted a family. It's a lonely life. Of course, I later ended up being in solitary confinement [as a POW]." He chuckles at the irony. "Being a priest is just a lonely life and I couldn't see myself as one." He obviously listened to himself.

Dick continued to listen in Vietnam. After a while, he said, he and his fellow captives became tired of locker-room talk. He found himself leading the more philosophical, intellectual discussions and guiding the banter to a more esoteric level. They all knew exercising the mind was as important to staying healthy as physical exercise was. Besides, he had always liked philosophy. It reminded him of flying.

"For me, theology and philosophy are to living as the aircraft flight envelope is to flying. In the world of flying, each individual aircraft has a flight envelope that takes into consideration all aspects of energy and configuration: weight, G loading, angle of bank and pitch, air speed, acceleration, and deceleration. In

the world of living, there is [also] a human performance envelope, which is defined by theology and philosophy—natural law or religious law and logic. If an individual chooses to live outside this envelope, it is his right as a creature of free will. [But] the individual must be held accountable and bear the consequences of his actions. It is in effect the ultimate exercise of intellectual integrity and moral freedom."

St. Thomas Aquinas is Dick's favorite philosopher, the ultimate creature of free will. As he puts it, "St. Thomas built a better flight envelope in that he had a format: 'They say, I say,' and a choice of words and idea—clarity, rationality, succinctness, alternatives, and structure—that could be clearly understood by the end user. He wrote for pilots."

After retiring from the Navy, Dick made listening a full-time job. He followed in his wife's footsteps and pursued a master's degree in social work. He became a therapist. Alice has been a counselor for more than forty years, well recognized in her field—even serving as a political appointee in the Reagan Administration, overseeing family service issues for the Pentagon. They both recently retired as contract counselors for the Navy and now devote themselves to their grandchildren.

With a dry, sarcastic wit—usually accompanied by a devilish smirk and a still-strong Bostonian accent—Dick has chiseled, hawk-like features that have filled out and softened over the years. Granddaughters have a way of doing that to a man. For Dick, spending time with the girls in his life makes up for the seven years he lost with his own three sons. "Children are gifts from God— only on loan to the parent."

# *I Won't*

## THE HONORABLE ORSON G. SWINDLE III,
### FEDERAL TRADE COMMISSIONER AND LIEUTENANT COLONEL, USMC (RET.)

*T*he resistance started early in life.

When his folks divorced after World War II and went their separate ways, Orson Swindle refused to leave his hometown of Camilla, Georgia, and demanded that he stay and be raised by his grandmother and great aunt. "I said, 'I'm not leaving Camilla, Georgia.' Here I am making decisions at nine years old," he says, surprising even himself. "I didn't want to leave my friends and I said, 'I'm just not goin' to go.'"

Instead, he stayed in his small hometown of four thousand people, living the life of "a little South Georgia boy, runnin' around barefoot." He spent his summers without air conditioning, sleeping with his head resting on a pillow perched in an open window, keeping cool with books and a radio—his outlets to the world. He listened to baseball, prizefights, the Green Hornet, Jack Benny, the "Inner Sanctum," and accounts of World War II battles. He longed to be a part of the action.

So Orson headed to Atlanta and Georgia Tech and then the Marine Corps. It's hard to know if the Marine Corps standard gave him the tough inner core for which he is famous or if his resolute personality made him a natural fit for the Corps. He headed to Vietnam soon after and was shot down during his 205th mission on Veteran's Day 1966.

His friend and fellow inmate in the Hanoi Hilton, retired Air Force Col. George McKnight, described Orson's determination as a POW in a speech: "The door was flung open with a crash and into our world stumbled one very strange-looking human being. To put it briefly and mildly, he was filthy. From head to toe, he was filthy. Even by our admittedly low standards of personal hygiene, he was filthy. We waited until the guards left the room before welcoming him to our humble abode. The cell door had no sooner banged shut than he introduced himself to us: 'Captain Orson Swindle, United States Marine Corps' . . . and then he apologized for his unkempt appearance. 'The camp authorities wanted me to sign my name on a form for soap and a toothbrush. I, of course, refused.' . . . Something was obvious to us. The Marines had landed in the Hanoi Hilton and the performance bar had just been  raised."

When he retired from the Marine Corps, Orson couldn't sit still. He held several Reagan administration posts, served as Ross Perot's spokesman in his 1992 presidential bid, and twice ran unsuccessfully for Congress from Hawaii. Fiercely optimistic and insistent that he be involved, he sought out another chal-

lenge and found it—once again—in public service. Now, as one of five politically appointed federal trade commissioners, Orson finds himself in a world of lawyers and economists, and he is neither.

"I have to run a little faster than everyone else. Things don't always go my way and I get my head knocked every now and then, but I just love the fray." Sometimes, he finds himself alone on the other side of an issue. "'Orson,' my peers have argued, 'you're gonna stand alone on this decision.' I say, 'So what? I've been there before!'"

For Orson, resisting is a matter of both survival and pride. Sitting inconspicuously on a side table in his office is a small portrait of a Scottish prisoner being interrogated by the Huns. The artwork has a simple title: *I won't.*

# *Biographical Information*

## Everett Alvarez Jr.

*Military Rank:* Commander, USN (Ret.)

*Age When Captured:* 26

*Total Number of Days Held in Captivity in Vietnam:* 3,113

*Notable Military Citations/Awards:* Silver Star, two Legions of Merit with combat "V," Distinguished Flying Cross, two Bronze Stars with combat "V," two Purple Heart medals, and POW medal

A city park and two housing projects in California and Texas have been named in honor of Commander Alvarez. In January 1987, his hometown of Salinas, California, named a new high school in his honor. In 1998, he was awarded the Daughters of the American Revolution's Medal of Honor. The U.S. Congress named a Rockville, Maryland, post office in his honor in 2000. Commander Alvarez has also been given the distinguished honor of being named the Rotary Club's National "Citizen of the Year" award.

The University of Santa Clara has given him the Alumnus of Distinction Award, as well as an honorary doctorate in Public Service. In May 2001, he was awarded another honorary doctorate from the University of North Texas Health Science Center.

*February 12, 1973.*
*Lt. Cdr. Everett Alvarez Jr., the longest-*

*Residence:* Potomac, Maryland

*held POW in North Vietnam, was the first in line to board the AC-141A Starlifter Cargo Transport Aircraft at Gia Lam Airport in Hanoi, North Vietnam.*

*Current Occupation:* Business owner, presidential appointee

Photo courtesy of the U.S. Navy.

*Marital Status:* Married to Thomasine "Tammy" Ilyas Alvarez

*Children:* 2

*Grandchildren:* None

# Biography:

*The Alvarez family in their Maryland home, May 1993. Left to right: Marc, Tammy, Everett, Bryan.*
Photo courtesy of the Alvarez family.

A distinguished naval officer, government executive, and entrepreneur, Commander Alvarez is best known to the public as the first aviator shot down and captured in North Vietnam on August 5, 1964. After retiring from the Navy, Commander Alvarez was appointed by President Reagan as deputy director of the Peace Corps and then as deputy administrator of the Veterans Administration—both of which appointments received Senate confirmation. After leaving the government, Commander Alvarez was named vice president for government services for the Hospital Corporation of America.

In 1987, he formed his own consulting company, Conwal Inc., in McLean, Virginia, with more than three hundred employees. In 2005, he formed Alvarez and Associates and is the CEO and president. He also remains Of Counsel to Conwal Inc.

He holds a bachelor of science degree in electrical engineering from the University of Santa Clara, a master's degree in operations research and systems analysis from the Naval Postgraduate School, and a juris doctorate from the George Washington University School of Law. He is the Chairman of the Board of Regents of the Uniformed Services University of the Health Sciences (USUHS) and is a member of the President's Task Force to Improve Health Care Delivery for our Nation's Veterans. He was appointed Chairman of the CARES Commission (Capital Asset Realignment and Enhancement Study Commission). He sits on the Board of Directors of the National Graduate University and is a lifetime member of the Board of Fellows of Santa Clara University. Commander Alvarez has served on the White House Fellows Selection Committee and on numerous other nonprofit and university organizations.

He is the author of two books, *Chained Eagle* and *Code of Conduct.*

# William D. Beekman

*Military Rank:* Colonel, USAF (Ret.)

*Age When Captured:* 25

*Total Number of Days Held in Captivity in Vietnam:* 277

*Military Citations/Awards:* Distinguished Flying Cross with one oak leaf cluster, Bronze Star, Purple Heart with one oak leaf cluster, Meritorious Service Medal with two oak leaf clusters, Air Medal with one silver and three oak leaf clusters, Air Force Commendation Medal with one oak leaf cluster, Air Force Achievement Medal, Distinguished Presidential Unit Citation, Air Force Outstanding Unit Award with valor and one silver oak leaf cluster, POW Medal, and many other awards

*Residence:* Dayton, Ohio

*Current Occupation:* Retired

*Marital Status:* Married to Donna Beekman

*Children:* 3

*Grandchildren:* None

*Colonel Beekman at his retirement from the U.S. Air Force on December 7, 1987. Left to right: Katy, Colonel Beekman, Brian.*
Photo courtesy of the Department of Defense.

# Biography:

Upon returning from Vietnam, Colonel Beekman resumed his Air Force career, serving in increasingly responsible roles, at the Air Force Weapons Laboratory as an operations officer squadron commander, and at the Air Force Headquarters as the chief of the nuclear branch, RDT&E Requirements, where he revised regulations and directives to significantly expand the scope and requirements of the Air Force Survivability program. He was instrumental in creating and promulgating an integrated space defense concept that has become SDI.

He retired from the Air Force in 1987 and went to work as a management consultant for Booz Allen Hamilton Inc. creating libraries and computer databases for the Department of Defense. In 1992, he founded and directed a new corporation, Pulma Labs Inc., growing the company to a total of fifty-five employees—including forty offices operating throughout ten states. As the CEO, Colonel Beekman was responsible for managing the overall corporate operations, overseeing and training the administration and billing staff, and personally performing marketing, payroll, financial, and tax preparation duties. He sold the company in 2003 and retired.

Colonel Beekman holds a bachelor of science degree in astronautics from the U.S. Air Force Academy, a master of arts in management degree from Webster College in St. Louis, Missouri, and a master of science in astronautical engineering degree from the Air Force Institute of Technology at Wright-Patterson Air Force Base, Ohio.

*Colonel and Donna Beekman's wedding day, December 5, 1998.*
Photo courtesy of Colonel Beekman.

*Colonel Beekman embracing his mother, Geneva, upon his return home in March 1973.* Photo courtesy of the U.S. Air Force.

# George T. Coker

*Military Rank:* Commander, USN (Ret.)

*Age When Captured:* 23

*Total Number of Days Held in Captivity in Vietnam:* 2,382

*Military Citations/Awards:* Navy Cross, Silver Star, Legion of Merit with combat "V," Distinguished Flying Cross, two Bronze Stars with combat "V," two Purple Heart medals, Meritorious Service Medal, five Air Medals, three Navy Commendations with combat "V," and POW Medal

*Residence:* Virginia Beach, Virginia

*Current Occupation:* Retired

*Marital Status:* Married to Pamela Ann Coker

*Children:* 3

*Grandchildren:* None

*With wife Pam by his side, Lieutenant Commander Coker is awarded the Navy Cross and other medals in December 1974 at Naval Air Station North Island, Coronado, California.* Photo courtesy of NAS N.I., San Diego.

# Biography:

After returning from Vietnam, Commander Coker returned to active duty as a naval flight officer. He served in several attack squadrons and on the USS *Enterprise* and USS *Nimitz*. His final assignment was as the director of the Atlantic Fleet Command Center at the Atlantic Fleet headquarters in Norfolk, Virginia. He retired from the Navy in 1986 and worked in the mortgage banking business for several years before accepting a position as a computer analyst for the federal government. He retired in July 2002.

Commander Coker attended Rutgers University and obtained a bachelor of arts degree through a college completion course. He is active with the Boy Scouts as a scoutmaster. Both he and his wife are active volunteers with Engaged Encounter, a marriage preparation retreat program.

*The Coker family in 1983.*
Photo courtesy of
Commander Coker.

*Lieutenant Commander
Coker returns to active
duty. He reported to
VA-42 at Naval Air Station
Oceana, Virginia,
in August 1973.*
Photo courtesy of
Commander Coker.

# Thomas E. Collins

*Military Rank:* Lieutenant Colonel, USAF (Ret.)

*Age When Captured:* 26

*Total Number of Days Held in Captivity in Vietnam:* 2,674

*Military Citations/Awards:* Two Silver Stars, Legion of Merit, Bronze Star, two Purple Heart medals, and POW Medal

*Residence:* Lauderdale, Mississippi

*Current Occupation:* Retired

*Marital Status:* Married to Donnie Collins

*Children:* 2 (His second son, who was a medical doctor, died of hepatitis at age thirty-four.)

*Grandchildren:* 4

*Major Collins being returned to U.S. Air Force officers, Hanoi, February 12, 1973.* Photo courtesy of Lieutenant Colonel Collins.

# Biography:

After returning from Vietnam, Lieutenant Colonel Collins finished his Air Force career, retiring in 1979. He then served as the executive director of the Veterans' Agency in Mississippi for seven years.

He was the Republican nominee for Congress from the fourth district of Mississippi in 1988 and served as an assistant secretary of labor under President Bush in 1989–1992.

Since 1993, Lieutenant Colonel Collins has been active in political, financial, and governmental affairs in his home state of Mississippi.

He holds a bachelor's degree in business from Mississippi State University and a master of business administration degree from the University of Southern Mississippi.

Max, one of the Collins's beloved bull dogs, died in 2005.

*Major Collins, 34, with his Freedom Flight 157 instructor of the 560th Squadron at Randolph Air Force Base in San Antonio, Texas, in 1974. This was his first flight after returning from Hanoi.* Photo courtesy of Randolph Air Force Base.

*The Collins family at their home in Hattiesburg, Mississippi, 1974. Left to right: Major Collins, Ted, Donnie, Marty, the dog, Ranger.* Photo courtesy of Lieutenant Colonel Collins.

# Render Crayton

*Military Rank:* Captain, USN (Ret.)

*Age When Captured:* 33

*Total Number of Days Held in Captivity in Vietnam:* 2,562

*Military Citations/Awards:* Distinguished Service Medal, three Silver Star medals, one Legion of Merit, five Bronze Star medals, two Purple Heart medals, Meritorious Service Medal, eighteen Air Medals, and POW Medal

*Residence:* Sun Valley, Idaho

*Current Occupation:* Retired

*Marital Status:* Married to Fern MacKenzie in 2003

*Children:* 1

*Grandchildren:* None

*Captain Crayton and his mother, Mary Jane Crayton, at her ninetieth birthday party in 1994. Photo courtesy of Captain Crayton.*

# Biography:

Upon returning from Vietnam, Captain Crayton returned to active duty in naval aviation. He served as chief of staff at the Naval War College in Newport, Rhode Island, as commander of naval activities, Spain—headquartered in Rota— and as the first commanding officer of the Naval ROTC unit in San Diego.

After retiring from the Navy with thirty years of service, Captain Crayton worked as the vice president of administration for a large holding company head-quartered in La Jolla, California. He has now retired to Sun Valley, Idaho, to pursue real estate investments.

Captain Crayton holds a bachelor's degree from the Georgia Institute of Tech-nology and a master of business administration from San Diego State University.

His beloved mother died in 2003.

*Captain Crayton and his son, Doug, in Sun Valley, Idaho, home in 2004.* Photo courtesy of the Crayton family.

*Captain Crayton with his wife of two years, Fern Mackenzie, vacationing in San Francisco, California, in 2002.* Photo courtesy of Captain Crayton.

# George E. "Bud" Day

*Military Rank:* Colonel, USAF (Ret.)

*Age When Captured:* 42

*Total Number of Days Held in Captivity in Vietnam:* 2,067 (less escape—about 18 days)

*Military Citations/Awards:* Medal of Honor, Air Force Cross, Distinguished Service Medal, Silver Star, Legion of Merit, Distinguished Flying Cross, Bronze Star for Valor with two oak leaf clusters, Purple Heart medal with three clusters, Air Medal with nine oak leaf clusters, and POW Medal.

Colonel Day was also presented Vietnam's highest medal by President Thieu, two Vietnamese Gallantry Crosses, and Vietnamese wings. He wears twelve campaign battle stars.

An airfield at the Sioux City, Iowa, Gateway Airport, and the Survival School Building at Fairchild Air Force Base have been named in his honor.

*Residence:* Shalimar, Florida

*Current Occupation:* Lawyer in private practice, advocate for veteran's health care

*Marital Status:* Married to Doris M. "Dorie" Day (aka "Viking")

*Children:* 4

*Grandchildren:* 12

*Bud Day sitting in the cockpit of his 84-F while stationed in Weathersfield, England, 1956. Photo courtesy of Tom Blau.*

# Biography:

The most highly decorated officer since Gen. Douglas MacArthur, Colonel Day retired from the military as one of its most experienced jet fighter pilots, with more than 4,500 hours of single jet time and more than 5,000 hours of flying time. He has flown all of the modern Air Force jet fighters. Since retiring from the military, Colonel Day has started his own private law practice and has waged a class-action lawsuit to restore health care benefits to military retirees over the age of sixty-five.

While the Supreme Court would not hear Colonel Day's case in 2003, he is now spearheading an effort change the law through the "Keep Our Promise to America's Retirees Act," reintroduced in the U.S. House of Representatives in January 2005.

Colonel Day is active in his local community, having served in leadership positions in numerous political, civic, and military organizations. He has also taught several college-level law and history classes and received the 1988 Business Associate of the Year award from the American Business Women's Association.

Colonel Day holds a bachelor of science degree and a doctor of humane letters from Morningside College in Sioux City, Iowa, a master of arts degree from St. Louis University, a juris doctorate from the University of South Dakota, and a doctor of laws degree from Troy State University. He was admitted to the South Dakota Bar in 1949 and the Florida Bar in 1977.

Colonel Day has published numerous articles on fighter performance, articles in the *Saturday Evening Post* and *Air Force Magazine*, and his autobiography, *Return With Honor*.

*The Day family gathered in Sioux City, Iowa, for the Sioux City Airport dedication. The airport was renamed Colonel Bud Day Field on May 25, 2002.* Photo courtesy of Colonel Day.

# Jeremiah A. Denton Jr.

*Military Rank:* Rear Admiral, USN (Ret.)

*Age When Captured:* 41

*Total Number of Days Held in Captivity in Vietnam:* 2,766

*Military Citations/Awards:* Navy Cross, Defense Distinguished Service Medal, Navy Distinguished Service Medal, three Silver Stars, Distinguished Flying Cross, five Bronze Stars, two Air Medals, two Purple Heart medals, and POW Medal

*Residence:* Theodore, Alabama

*Current Occupation:* Founded and runs nonprofit organization

*Marital Status:* Married to Jane Maury Denton

*Children:* 7

*Grandchildren:* 16 + 1 great-grandchild

*Rear Adm. Jeremiah Denton while serving as commandant of the Armed Forces Staff College in Norfolk, Virginia, 1975.*
Photo courtesy of Rear Admiral Denton.

# Biography:

After returning from Vietnam, Rear Admiral Denton was promoted to Rear Admiral and served as the commandant of the Armed Forces Staff College in Norfolk, Virginia. Upon retirement, he returned to his native Alabama and was elected to the U.S. Senate in November 1980. Among his many other legislative accomplishments, Rear Admiral Denton established the highly acclaimed international aid program now known as the Denton Program. Following his Senate term, he was appointed in 1987 by President Reagan to be chairman of the Presidential Commission on Merchant Marine and Defense.

He has since founded the Rear Adm. Jeremiah Denton Foundation and a humanitarian aid program known as TRANSFORM (Transportation for the Relief of Mankind). Rear Admiral Denton holds a bachelor of science degree from the U.S. Naval Academy. He lectures on national and international affairs while serving as a member of numerous college boards of directors. He is the coauthor of *When Hell Was in Session*, which was published and made into an NBC television movie.

*President Reagan signing a bill in the 1980s authored*
*by senator Denton and passed by congress.*
Photo courtesy of Rear Admiral Denton.

# John C. "Jack" Ensch

*Military Rank:* Captain, USN (Ret.)

*Age When Captured:* 34

*Total Number of Days Held in Captivity in Vietnam:* 216

*Military Citations/Awards:* Navy Cross, three Legions of Merit, two Bronze Stars with combat "V," two Purple Heart medals, three Meritorious Service Medals, eighteen Air Medals, three Navy Commendation Medals with combat "V," Combat Action Ribbon, Presidential Unit Citation, two Navy Unit Commendations, Meritorious Unit Commendation, POW Medal, Navy Expeditionary Medal, two National Defense Service Medals, two Armed Forces Expeditionary Medals, three Sea Service Deployment Ribbons, Republic of Vietnam (RVN) Service Medal (with one Silver and three Bronze Stars), RVN Honor Medal (1st class), RVN Gallantry Cross Medal (with Gold Star), RVN Gallantry Cross Unit Citation, RVN Campaign Medal

Captain Ensch was inducted into the Sacred Heart–Griffin High School Hall of Fame in 1998 in Springfield, Illinois.

*Residence:* San Diego, California

*Current Occupation:* Director of Military Marketing, San Diego Padres

*Marital Status:* Married to Kathy Ensch

*Children:* 3

*Grandchildren:* 4

*The Ensch family at Balboa Naval Hospital, 1973.*
*Left to right: Chris (2), Kathy, Jack, Becky (5), Beth (8).*
Photo courtesy of Captain Ensch.

# Biography:

When he returned from Vietnam, Captain Ensch spent nine months in rehabilitation. He then resumed his Navy career and served with distinction in many jobs with increasing responsibility, including stints as the executive officer of the Navy Fighter Weapons School (TOPGUN) at Naval Air Station Miramar; commanding officer of Fighter Squadron 114; commanding officer of Naval Air Station, Key West; inspector general of the Naval Education and Training Command in Pensacola, Florida; and the last commanding officer of the Naval Training Center, San Diego.

He retired from the Navy in 1995 and was recruited by the Padres to serve as their first director of military marketing. Among his accomplishments with the Padres are the annual Military Home Opener, selling a total of 300,000 discounted military tickets, hosting some 60,000 Marine recruits, having thirty player caravans visit military bases, having eight players make at-sea visits to ships, having two Little Padres Parks constructed in military housing areas (Murphy Canyon and Camp Pendleton), and issuing lifetime passes to World War II and Korea POWs.

Captain Ensch holds a bachelor's degree from Illinois State University and a master's degree in systems management from the University of Southern California. He is also a graduate of the Industrial College of the Armed Forces in Washington, D.C.

*Capt. Jack Ensch at the start of the Blue Angel Marathon in 1993 at Naval Air Station, Pensacola, Florida. This was his seventh marathon—on the tenth anniversary of his release from Hanoi. In 1998, at the age of sixty, Captain Ensch ran his eighth and last marathon, the first San Diego Rock 'n' Roll Marathon.* Photo courtesy of Captain Ensch.

*Capt. Jack Ensch's change of command and retirement celebration at the Naval Training Center, San Diego, California, June 1995. Left to right: Chris, Kathy, Captain Ensch, Becky, Beth.* Photo courtesy of Captain Ensch.

# John H. Fellowes

*Military Rank:* Captain, USN (Ret.)

*Age When Captured:* 34

*Total Number of Days Held in Captivity in Vietnam:* 2,381

*Military Citations/Awards:* Silver Star, two Legions of Merit, Distinguished Flying Cross, three Bronze Stars, two Purple Heart medals, five Air Medals, two Navy Commendation Medals, and POW Medal

*Residence:* Annapolis, Maryland

*Current Occupation:* Retired, volunteer

*Marital Status:* Married to Patricia Watkins Fellowes

*Children:* 4

*Grandchildren:* 4

*The Fellowes family in March 1973. Left to right: Sharon, Pat, Tom, Captain Fellowes, John, Cathy.* Photo courtesy of Captain Fellowes.

# Biography:

After returning from Vietnam, Captain Fellowes returned to active duty and retired in 1986 after thirty years of naval service. Since retirement, he has taught at the U.S. Naval Academy and works at the Maryland State Legislature. In 2001, Captain Fellowes was awarded the title of honorary chief petty officer under the hand of the master chief petty officer of the Navy, Master Chief Jim Herdt.

Captain Fellowes holds a bachelor's degree from the U.S. Naval Academy and is a graduate of the National Defense University.

*Fellowes's promotion to captain, 1984.*
Photo courtesy of the Department of Defense.

*Captain Fellowes and Pat Fellowes are reunited on March 7, 1973, at Portsmouth Naval Hospital after nearly seven years of separation.*
Photo courtesy of the Department of Defense.

# Paul E. Galanti

*Military Rank:* Commander, USN (Ret.)

*Age When Captured:* 26

*Total Number of Days Held in Captivity in Vietnam:* 2,432

*Military Citations/Awards:* Silver Star, two Legions of Merit for combat, Bronze Star for combat, two Purple Heart medals, Meritorious Service Medal, nine Air Medals, and Navy Commendation Medal for combat

*Residence:* Richmond, Virginia

*Current Occupation:* Consultant, political activist, public speaker, veterans' advocate

*Marital Status:* Married to Phyllis Galanti

*Children:* 2

*Grandchildren:* None

*Lt. Paul Galanti, 26, as a prisoner of war in North Vietnam, attempting to show defiance against the Vietnamese propaganda by pointing his two middle fingers toward the ground. The image was used on the cover of* Life *magazine in 1967; however, the middle fingers were airbrushed out.*
Photo courtesy of Commander Galanti.

# Biography:

Following repatriation, Commander Galanti served as the Navy's chief-recruiter in Virginia and as a battalion officer at the U.S. Naval Academy. After retiring from the Navy, he became the first non-pharmacist executive director of the Virginia Pharmaceutical Association, the CEO of the Medical Society of Virginia, and the executive director of the Science Museum of Virginia Foundation. He also headed up marketing for Eye-Q, LLC, a web application developer.

During the 2000 presidential primaries, Commander Galanti was the Virginia chair of Senator John McCain's presidential bid. He served on the Secretary of Veterans Affairs' Advisory Committee on Former POWs and currently serves on the board of the Virginia governor's new Department of Veterans' Services. Commander Galanti has given inspirational messages to more than thirteen hundred groups.

He holds a bachelor of science degree from the U.S. Naval Academy and a master of commerce from the University of Richmond.

*The Galanti family attending the thirtieth anniversary POW reunion in Anaheim, California, in 2003. Left to right: Jamie, Phyllis, Commander Galanti, Jeff.* Photo courtesy of the Galanti family.

# Douglas B. Hegdahl

*Military Rank:* Seaman, U.S. Navy

*Age When Captured:* 20

*Total Number of Days Held in Captivity in Vietnam:* 852

*Military Citations/Awards:* Purple Heart medal, POW Medal, National Defense Service Medal, Vietnam Service Medal

Upon his retirement from civil service in 2001, Mr. Hegdahl was given the Civilian Meritorious Service award.

*Residence:* San Diego, California

*Current Occupation:* Retired

*Marital Status:* Single

*Children:* None

*Grandchildren:* None

*In 1967, shortly after Seaman Apprentice Hegdahl, 20, was captured, this image was taken by the Vietnamese. Hegdahl actually had a swollen lip, but the Vietnamese retouched the image so he did not appear hurt.* Photo courtesy of the Department of Defense.

# Biography:

At the urging of his fellow POWs and a direct order from his senior ranking officer, Mr. Hegdahl took an early release from captivity in August 1969. The names he memorized were valuable intelligence for the U.S. government on the fate of many MIAs and POWs. His information was comfort to many families. He was recruited by Ross Perot and several POW wives to physically confront the North Vietnamese Peace Talk Delegation about the fate of the missing in action. He appeared on the Dick Cavett Show with Sybil Stockdale, Vice Admiral Stockdale's wife, and helped her in the cause to bring home the rest of the POWs.

He entered the Civil Service and spent thirty years as a survival school instructor for the U.S. Navy and the James B. Stockdale Survival, Evasion, Resistance, and Escape Center (SERE), at Naval Air Station, North Island, Coronado, California. He retired in 2001.

Mr. Hegdahl has two brothers who live in Seattle and Sioux Falls, South Dakota. He is still a local hero when he returns to his hometown of Clark, South Dakota. He rides his bikes several miles a day, and he finally took that trip to Australia in 2005.

*Doug Hegdahl being presented with a plaque at his retirement party in North Island, Coronado, California, September 2001. Mr. Hegdahl became an instructor at the Survival Evasion Resistance Escape School (SERE School) upon his return from Vietnam. Mr. Hegdahl is kneeling on the floor and Vice Admiral Stockdale is standing in the center of the image.*
Photo courtesy of Mr. Hegdahl.

*Petty Officer Third Class Doug Hegdahl, September 3, 1969, riding with his mother, Edith, and father, Abe, in his welcome home parade.* Photo courtesy of Mr. Hegdahl.

# James L. "Duffy" Hutton

*Military Rank:* Captain, USN (Ret.)

*Age When Captured:* 33

*Total Number of Days Held in Captivity in Vietnam:* 2,676

*Notable Military Citations Awards:* Silver Star, Legion of Merit with combat "V," Distinguished Flying Cross, Bronze Star with combat "V," Purple Heart medal with two Gold Stars, Air Medal with two Bronze Stars, Navy Commendation Medal with combat "V," Combat Action Ribbon, Navy Unit Commendation, POW Medal, National Defense Service Medal, Armed Forces Expeditionary Medal, Vietnam Service Medal, Republic of Vietnam Campaign Medal (13 campaigns), and Vietnam Meritorious Unit Citation

*Residence:* La Jolla, California

*Current Occupation:* Retired

*Marital Status:* Married to Eileen Hutton

*Children:* 1

*Grandchildren:* 1

*Commander Hutton returns to the U.S. military control at Gia Lam Airfield in Hanoi, North Vietnam, on February 12, 1973.*
Photo courtesy of the Department of Defense.

# Biography:

After returning from Vietnam and a period of physical rehabilitation, Captain Hutton returned to full active duty in the Navy. He retired as the executive officer of the Navy Drug Rehabilitation Center at Naval Air Station, Miramar, California.

Captain Hutton worked as a residential real estate agent in San Diego for ten years. During that time, he served as the vice president for military relocations for Prudential Dunn. He was an active member of the La Jolla Kiwanis for several years and volunteered as an aid in a special education class at All Hallows School in La Jolla.

Captain Hutton holds a bachelor of science degree in education from the Wilson Teachers College and a master's degree from the U.S. International University (USIU). He and his wife Eileen are now fully retired and frequently travel to Florida to visit their grandson, Hunter.

His poems are on permanent display at the Smithsonian's National Museum of American History in "The Price of Freedom" exhibit.

*Commander Hutton embraces his mother, Alma Fugitt, and his sister, Mary, upon his return to Miramar Naval Air Station in San Diego, California, on February 16, 1973.* Photo courtesy of Captain Hutton.

*Capt. Duffy Hutton enjoying an afternoon in the San Diego Zoo with his nine-month-old grandson, James Hunter Hutton, August 26, 2004.* Photo courtesy of Captain Hutton.

# Samuel R. Johnson

*Military Rank:* Colonel, USAF (Ret.)

*Age When Captured:* 35

*Total Number of Days Held in Captivity in Vietnam:* 2,494

*Military Citations/Awards:* Two Silver Stars, two Legions of Merit, the Distinguished Flying Cross, one Bronze Star with Valor, two Purple Heart medals, four Air Medals, and three Outstanding Unit awards

*Residence:* Plano, Texas, and Washington, D.C.

*Current Occupation:* U.S. Representative

*Marital Status:* Married to Shirley Melton Johnson

*Children:* 3

*Grandchildren:* 10 + 2 great-grandchildren

*Major Johnson reunited with his family at Sheppard Air Force Base in Wichita Falls, Texas, on February 17, 1973.*
Photo courtesy of the U.S. Air Force.

# Biography:

Congressman Johnson returned home to Texas after serving in the Air Force for twenty-nine years as a highly decorated pilot. He established a home-building business and served in the Texas State Legislature. In 1991, he was elected to represent the people of the third district of Texas in the U.S. Congress.

Dubbed a "Top Texan" by *USA Today*, he is the highest ranking Texan on both the House Ways and Means Committee and the Committee on Education and Workforce. As one of the few members of Congress who have fought in combat, he also serves as an informal adviser on military readiness issues.

Congressman Johnson holds a bachelor's degree from Southern Methodist University. He is the author of *Captive Warrior,* a memoir about his experience in Vietnam.

*Colonel Johnson sitting on the wing of his F-86 in Korea in 1953. Named for his wife, "Shirley's Texas Tornado" ferried him on sixty-two combat missions.* Photo courtesy of the Department of Defense.

*Congressman Johnson and his wife, Shirley Johnson, on Capitol Hill in 2004.* Photo courtesy of the Office of Representative Johnson.

# Floyd Harold "Hal" Kushner, MD, FACS

*Military Rank:* Colonel, USA (Ret.)

*Age When Captured:* 26

*Total Number of Days Held in Captivity in Vietnam:* 1,933

*Military Citations/Awards:* Silver Star, Soldiers' Medal, Bronze Star, three Air Medals, three Purple Heart medals, Army Commendation Medal, Republic of Vietnam Cross of Gallantry with Palm, Republic of Vietnam Campaign Ribbon (with ten battle stars), two Presidential Unit Citations, POW Medal, Armed Forces Reserve Achievement Medal, Combat Medics badge, Senior Flight Surgeon's Badge, eleven overseas stripes

*Major Kushner returns to the U.S. military control in Hanoi, North Vietnam, on March 16, 1973.* Photo courtesy of the Department of Defense.

In 1973, Colonel Kushner was named the Military Flight Surgeon of the Year, and in 1990, by order of the secretary of the Army, he was made a permanent "Distinguished Member of the 9th Cavalry Regiment." In 2001, he was inducted into the Army Aviation Hall of Fame, and the outpatient dispensary of 9th Cavalry of 1st Cavalry Division at Fort Hood, Texas, was named for him and dedicated to him. He gave the commencement address to the Tripler Army Medical Center in 2005, the hospital in which he was born and where he interned twenty-five years later.

*Residence:* Daytona Beach, Florida

*Current Occupation:* Ophthalmologist, volunteer surgeon with various charitable foundations

*Marital Status:* Married to Gayle Freeman in 2005

*Children:* 2

*Grandchildren:* 3

# Biography:

Upon returning to the United States, Dr. Kushner continued his Army medical career in internal medicine and ophthalmology until his retirement in 1986. Since 1977, Dr. Kushner has worked in private practice as an ophthalmologist in Daytona Beach, Florida. He also participates in humanitarian medical missions and has traveled to Peru, Turkey, India, and Tanzania as a visiting surgeon.

He has served on the board of the YMCA for many years and has served as the president of its Daytona Board and the Y Metro Board. He has been chief of staff at Halifax Hospital and has served as chairman of most of its major committees.

He holds a bachelor of arts degree in chemistry with highest honors from the University of North Carolina in Chapel Hill and his medical degree from the Medical College of Virginia (MCV). While at MCV in Richmond, Virginia, Dr. Kushner won the Mosby Scholarship Award. He has served as keynote speaker to many military organizations and has published nine articles in various medical journals.

His beloved mother died in 2002.

*Col. Hal Kushner and his wife Gayle in Dallas, Texas, for the NAM-POW's twenty-fifth reunion in 1998.*
Photo courtesy of Colonel Kushner.

*Colonel Kushner on a charity medical mission to Tanzania, Africa, on July 14, 2002. He had just completed cataract surgery on one of the local men.*
Photo courtesy of Colonel Kushner.

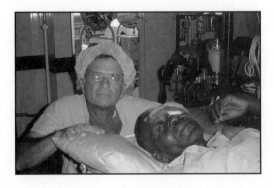

# William P. Lawrence

*Military Rank:* Vice Admiral, USN (Ret.)

*Age When Captured:* 37

*Total Number of Days Held in Captivity in Vietnam:* 2,076

*Military Citations/Awards:* Four Distinguished Service Medals, three Silver Stars, Legion of Merit, Distinguished Flying Cross, Bronze Star with combat "V," two Purple Heart medals, three Air Medals, Joint Service Commendation Medal, two Navy Commendation Medals with combat "V," and POW Medal

*William P. Lawrence, Midshipman First Class, Brigade Commander of the U.S. Naval Academy, 1951. Photo courtesy of the U.S. Naval Academy.*

The first naval aviator to fly twice the speed of sound in a Navy airplane, Vice Admiral Lawrence was a Navy nominee for the initial astronaut selection and was among the final thirty-two candidates for the Project Mercury program before being disqualified for a minor physical defect.

He also has received numerous athletic awards, including the National Football Foundation and College Hall of Fame Gold medal, the National Collegiate Athletic Association's 1984 Theodore Roosevelt Award, the Vice Adm. William P. Lawrence Award, an award given by the Navy to the most outstanding air traffic control maintenance technician in the Navy, the Navy League's Arleigh Burke Leaderhip award for outstanding leadership, personal integrity, professional achievement, and unselfish dedication to America.

*Residence:* Crownsville, Maryland

*Current Occupation:* Retired and writing his memoirs

*Marital Status:* Married to Diane Lawrence

*Children:* 4

*Grandchildren:* 5

*Vice Admiral and Mrs. Lawrence in honor of his departure as superintendent of the U.S. Naval Academy, August 1981. Photo courtesy of Vice Admiral Lawrence.*

**119**

# Biography:

Upon his return from Vietnam, Vice Admiral Lawrence served as Commander, Light Attack Wing, U.S. Pacific Fleet in Lemoore, California. Subsequently, he served as the director, Aviation Programs Division, and assistant deputy chief of naval operations (air warfare). He became superintendent of the U.S. Naval Academy in 1978, when his daughter was a midshipman (student) and one of the first class of women permitted to attend. Vice Admiral Lawrence then assumed command of the U.S. Third Fleet and then became the Navy's chief of personnel.

He retired from active duty in 1986 and subsequently occupied the Chair of Naval Leadership at the Naval Academy and served as the president of the Association of Naval Aviation. He was a visiting professional scholar at the Freedom Forum First Amendment Center at Vanderbilt University, conducting research and preparing a report on the relationship between the military and the media.

Vice Admiral Lawrence holds a bachelor's degree from the U.S. Naval Academy and an honorary doctor of humane letters degree from Fisk University in Nashville, Tennessee. He is affiliated with numerous business, athletic, and military organizations. His daughter, Wendy, is a U.S. Naval Academy graduate and a Navy pilot, currently serving as an astronaut. A veteran of three space flights, she has logged 894 hours in space and was a mission specialist on the Discovery flight in July 2005. She was the first woman naval aviator and Naval Academy graduate to fly in space. Vice Admiral Lawrence and his wife are retired and are writing their memoirs.

*Astronaut Wendy Lawrence, flight engineer and mission specialist for STS-67, is a 1981 graduate of the U.S. Naval Academy. Her father, Vice Admiral Lawrence, was superintendent of the U.S. Naval Academy when his daughter attended as a member of one of the first mixed-gender classes.* Photo courtesy of NASA.

# Tony Marshall

*Military Rank:* Lieutenant Colonel, USAF (Ret.)

*Age When Captured:* 25

*Total Number of Days Held in Captivity in Vietnam:* 269

*Military Citations/Awards:* Distinguished Flying Cross with four oak leaf clusters, Purple Heart medal, Meritorious Service Medal with three oak leaf clusters, Air Medal with sixteen oak leaf clusters, Air Force Commendation Medal, POW Medal, Vietnam Service medal, RVN Gallantry Cross, Air Force Outstanding Unit Award with Valor device and one oak leaf cluster, and Combat Readiness Medal

*Residence:* Apple Valley, California

*Current Occupation:* Commercial airline pilot, substitute high school teacher

*Marital Status:* Widowed (Wife of ten years, Veta Marshall, died of cancer November 2002)

*Children:* 1

*Grandchildren:* 1

# Biography:

After returning from Vietnam, Lieutenant Colonel Marshall continued flying in the Air Force and retired with 480 hours of combat flying time, 3,000 hours in the F-4, and 3,600 hours total flying time. Staff duties during his twenty-two-year career included flight commander, assistant operations officer, chief of training, chief of standardization and evaluation, and transportation squadron commander.

*Capt. Tony Marshall, 24, at Udorn Air Base, Thailand, in front of his F-4D plane, 1971.*
Photo courtesy of the Department of Defense.

Upon retirement from the Air Force, Lieutenant Colonel Marshall became a commercial pilot with United Airlines and is currently a captain on the A320 aircraft. When he is not flying, he substitute teaches in his local school district.

He holds a bachelor's degree in mathematics from the U.S. Air Force Academy and a master's degree in business management.

*Captain Marshall, 26, with his mom, Ann Marshall, at his homecoming reception at Andrews Air Force Base, March 29, 1973.* Photo courtesy of Lieutenant Colonel Marshall.

*Lieutenant Colonel Marshall dressed in his United Airlines uniform with his daughter Maria, 1991.* Photo courtesy of Lieutenant Colonel Marshall.

# Edward H. Martin

*Military Rank:* Vice Admiral, USN (Ret.)

*Age When Captured:* 36

*Total Number of Days Held in Captivity in Vietnam:* 2,066

*Military Citations/Awards:* Two Distinguished Service Medals, Silver Star, Defense Superior Service Medal, two Legions of Merit, Distinguished Flying Cross, two Bronze Stars, two Purple Heart medals, POW Medal, and National Order du Merite (France)

*Residence:* Coronado, California

*Current Occupation:* Public speaker, television commentator, serves on corporate and nonprofit boards

*Marital Status:* Married to Sharron H. "Sherry" Martin

*Children:* 3

*Grandchildren:* None

*Vice Admiral Martin while stationed in Italy as commander of the U.S. Sixth Fleet in 1984. He was invited to visit Vatican City for an official visit with Pope John Paul II to brief the pope on the prospects for stability and peace in the Mediterranean area.* Photo courtesy of the Vatican.

# Biography:

After returning from Vietnam, Vice Admiral Martin continued serving in the Navy as the commanding officer of a multi-commodity support ship, an aircraft carrier, and two carrier battle groups; commander of the U.S. 6th Fleet; commander of the NATO Striking and Support Forces in southern Europe; deputy chief of naval operations for air warfare; commander of the Eastern Atlantic; and deputy commander in chief of U.S. Naval Forces in Europe.

Vice Admiral Martin retired in 1989 from the Navy and became director of

European business development for the Xerox Corp. He founded E. H. Martin Associates and E. H. Martin Investments LP in 2000 to develop and manage small private properties, assets, and investments. He continues to serve on the boards of several financial-related corporations and numerous civic and educational pro bono boards of trustees, including the San Diego Maritime Museum, the U.S. Naval Academy Alumni Association, the U.S. Naval Academy Foundation, the U.S. Naval Aviation Museum Foundation, and the USS *Intrepid* museum. He is a former member of the board of advisors of the National Aeronautics and Space Museum (presidential appointee).

He holds a bachelor of science degree in engineering from the U.S. Naval Academy and a master's degree in international affairs from George Washington University. He is a distinguished graduate of the National War College and a graduate of the Naval War College.

*Vice Admiral Martin and his wife, Sherry*
*Martin, vacationing in Hawaii.*
Photo courtesy of Vice Admiral Martin.

# John S. McCain

*Military Rank:* Captain, USN (Ret.)

*Age When Captured:* 31

*Total Number of Days Held in Captivity in Vietnam:* 1,956

*Military Citations/Awards:* Silver Star, Legion of Merit, Distinguished Flying Cross, Bronze Star, Purple Heart medal, and POW Medal

*Residence:* Phoenix, Arizona, and Washington, D.C.

*Current Occupation:* U.S. Senator

*Marital Status:* Married to Cindy McCain

*Children:* 7

*Grandchildren:* 4

*Lt. Cdr. Jay Coupe (left) escorts Lt. Cdr. McCain to a waiting U.S. Air Force AC-141A Starlifter Cargo Transport aircraft at Gia Lam Airport in Hanoi, North Vietnam, March 14, 1973.* Photograph courtesy of the U.S. Navy.

# Biography:

After retiring from the Navy as a captain, Senator McCain was elected to Congress in 1982 as U.S. Representative from what was then the first congressional district of Phoenix, Arizona. In 1986, he was elected to the U.S. Senate to take the place of Senator Barry Goldwater. Senator McCain is currently the senior senator from Arizona.

He unsuccessfully ran for the Republican nomination for president of the United States in 2000. He is currently the chairman of the Senate Committee on Indian Affairs and serves on the Armed Services, and Commerce, Science and Transportation Committees.

*Commissioner Swindle and Senator McCain vacationing together with their families in the Republic of Palau in December 2003.* Photo taken by and courtesy of Angela Williams.

*Senator John McCain and President Ronald Reagan in discussion at the White House, Washington, D.C., 1986.* Photo courtesy of the office of Senator John McCain.

# John Michael McGrath

*Military Rank:* Captain, USN (Ret.)

*Age When Captured:* 27

*Total Number of Days Held in Captivity in Vietnam:* 2,074

*Military Citations/Awards:* Defense Superior Service Medal, two Legions of Merit with combat "V," two Distinguished Flying Crosses, Navy and Marine Corps Medal, three Bronze Stars with combat "V," two Purple Heart medals, seventeen Strike/Flight Air Medals, four Navy Commendation Medals with combat "V," and POW medal

Captain McGrath has also been elected to the National Wrestling Hall of Fame.

*Residence:* Monument, Colorado

*Current Occupation:* Retired

*Marital Status:* Married to Marlene McGrath

*Children:* 2

*Grandchildren:* 5

*Marlene pinning Lt. (j.g.) Mike McGrath with his Navy wings on November 22, 1963, thirty minutes before President Kennedy was shot. They were at Naval Air Station Beeville, Texas, just a few miles from Dallas. Just after the ceremony, they turned on their car radio to hear the news about Kennedy's assassination.* Photo courtesy of Captain McGrath.

# Biography:

After returning from Vietnam, Captain McGrath returned to active duty in naval aviation. He served as the commanding officer of VA-97, as chairman of the Leadership and Law Department at the U.S. Naval Academy, and as the naval attaché to Ecuador. He retired from the Navy in 1987 and became a commercial pilot for United Airlines. Captain McGrath retired from United in 1999.

He also published a book of drawings that graphically illustrated his experience as a POW. *Prisoner of War: Six Years in Hanoi* is in its eleventh printing and is available from the Naval Institute.

Captain McGrath holds a bachelor of science degree from the U.S. Naval Academy and a master of science degree in financial management from the Naval Postgraduate School in Monterey, California. He is active with the NAM-POW organization as the official historian and as a member of the board of directors.

*Captain McGrath's official photograph taken in March 1983, shortly before he reported to the U.S. embassy in Quito, Ecuador, where he served as naval attaché until October 1986.* Photo courtesy of the U.S. Navy.

*The McGrath family at their son Jay's wedding in July 1995. Left to right: Captain McGrath, Marlene, Jay, Rick.* Photo courtesy of Captain McGrath.

*The McGrath family portrait taken March 9, 1973, a few days after Captain McGrath's return home. Left to right: Captain McGrath, Marlene, Jay, Rick.* Photo courtesy of Captain McGrath.

# Edward J. Mechenbier

*Military Rank:* Major General, USAF (Ret.)

*Age When Captured:* 24

*Total Number of Days Held in Captivity in Vietnam:* 2,075

*Military Citations/Awards:* Distinguished Service Medal, Silver Star with one oak leaf cluster, Distinguished Flying Cross with cluster, Bronze Star with combat "V," Purple Heart medal with cluster, Air Medal with eight clusters, Air Force Commendation Medal, and POW Medal

*Residence:* Beavercreek, Ohio

*Current Occupation:* Business executive with SAIC

*Marital Status:* Married to Jerri Mechenbier

*Children:* 4

*Grandchildren:* 4

*Major General Mechenbier (left) and Maj. Rick Webster piloting the AC-141A Starlifter Cargo Transport Aircraft, also known as the "Flight to Freedom," in June 2004. This plane ferried the POWs home.* Photo courtesy of Major General Mechenbier.

# Biography:

Major General Mechenbier was the last Vietnam POW to retire from the service (in June 2004). Through more than forty years in military aviation, he flew the F-4C/D, the F-100, the A-7, and the C-141C. He also flew more than twenty other aircraft for familiarization flights, including the F-16, F-15, F/A-18, and the Soviet MiG-29. He is a command pilot with more than 3,600 flying hours. His last assignment was serving as the mobilization assistant to the commander, Air Force Materiel Command at Wright-Patterson Air Force Base in Ohio.

Major General Mechenbier works as a vice president for development with Science Applications International Corporation (SAIC). For the last twenty-five years, he has served as the television host and emcee for several major air shows throughout the country. Additionally, he served as a member of the Reserve Forces Policy Board for the Secretary of Defense (2001–2004).

*The Mechenbier family attending Major General Mechenbier's retirement party held in the Air Force Museum at Wright Patterson Air Force Base, June 2004. Left to right: Tai, Bernhard, Jerri, Major General Mechenbier, Mahli, Kari.*
Photo courtesy of Major General Mechenbier.

# Ernest M. "Mel" Moore Jr.

*Military Rank:* Captain, USN (Ret.)

*Age When Captured:* 38

*Total Number of Days Held in Captivity in Vietnam:* 2,185

*Military Citations/Awards:* Silver Star, Legion of Merit, Distinguished Flying Cross, Bronze Star, Purple Heart medal, Air Medal, Navy Commendation Medal, POW Medal, Korean Service Medal, and Vietnam Service Medal

*Residence:* Bethel Island, California

*Current Occupation:* Retired

*Marital Status:* Divorced

*Children:* 3

*Grandchildren:* 6

*The Moore family in Coronado, California, right after Mel's return home from Vietnam. Left to right: Michelle, Mel, Melissa, Chloe, Leslie, Woos the cat.*
Photo courtesy of Captain Moore.

# Biography:

After his return from Vietnam, Captain Moore continued his military career, serving on the staff of the U.S. Naval Air Forces, Pacific. He then served as the commanding officer of a troop transport ship, the *Paul Revere*, and the USS *New Orleans* (LPH-11). He retired from the Navy in 1979.

Captain Moore earned a bachelor's degree from the Naval Postgraduate School in Monterey, California, and a master's degree from National University and USIU. He sold his fishing cabin and reunited with his ex-wife, Chloe, in 2005.

*Captain Moore and Chloe Moore attending Vice Admiral*
*Stockdale's funeral in San Diego, July 2005.*
Photo courtesy of Captain Moore.

# Richard D. "Moon" Mullen

*Military Rank:* Captain, USN (Ret.)

*Age When Captured:* 36

*Total Number of Days Held in Captivity in Vietnam:* 2,249

*Military Citations/Awards:* Silver Star, Legion of Merit, three Bronze Stars, two Purple Heart medals, Air Medal, and POW Medal (among other decorations)

*Residence:* La Jolla, California

*Current Occupation:* Retired

*Marital Status:* Married to Peggy Mullen

*Children:* 2

*Grandchildren:* 5 + 5 step-grandchildren

# Biography:

Upon returning from Vietnam, Captain Mullen finished his military career, retired, and pursued careers in aerospace engineering and real estate. He served as president of the Kiwanis Club of La Jolla, California, and as the lieutenant governor for the Kiwanis International California/Nevada/Hawaii Division. He has been a deacon and elder for his church.

*Captain Mullen and Peggy Mullen's wedding day, June 18, 2000.*
Photo courtesy of Captain Mullen.

He holds a bachelor of arts degree in economics from San Diego State University.

*Capt. Moon Mullen fishing in Sitka, Alaska, for salmon and halibut with Capt. Everett Southwick and Capt. Bill Stark, 2001. Left to right: Capt. Moon Mullen, Capt. Everett Southwick, Capt. Bill Stark.* Photo courtesy of Captain Southwick.

# Ben M. Pollard

*Military Rank:* Colonel, USAF (Ret.)

*Age When Captured:* 35

*Total Number of Days Held in Captivity in Vietnam:* 2,120

*Military Citations/Awards:* Silver Star with bronze oak leaf cluster, Legion of Merit with bronze oak leaf cluster, Bronze Star with Valor and bronze oak leaf cluster, Purple Heart with bronze oak leaf cluster, Meritorious Service Medal, Air Medal, Air Force Commendation Medal with bronze oak leaf cluster, Air Force Presidential Unit Citations, POW medal, National Defense Service Medal, Vietnam Service Medal with one Silver Service Star and three Bronze Service Stars, RVN Gallantry Cross with Palm, RVN Campaign Medal, Combat Readiness Medal, Small Arms Expert Marksmanship Ribbon, Air Force Longevity Service Award Ribbon with silver oak leaf cluster, Air Force Outstanding Unit Award with two bronze oak leaf clusters and with Valor

The Pollard family's first Christmas together in their Colorado Springs home after Colonel Pollard's return from Vietnam in 1973. From left to right: Mark, Thai the dog, Colonel Pollard, Joan, Ginny. Photo courtesy of Colonel Pollard.

*Residence:* Poway, California

*Current Occupation:* Retired

*Marital Status:* Married to Joan H. Pollard

*Children:* 2

*Grandchildren:* 4

# Biography:

After returning from Vietnam, Colonel Pollard spent the remainder of his military career at the U.S. Air Force Academy. He taught aeronautics and was an instructor at the Survival, Evasion, Resistance, Escape (SERE) Program. He initiated the "Soaring for All" Cadets and "Parachuting for All" Cadets programs, successfully introducing gliding and parachuting to all students at the U.S. Air Force Academy. In addition, he served as commander of the USAFA Preparatory School, which academically prepared marginally qualified students for the Air Force Academy.

Colonel Pollard retired in 1981 and became vice president of STARNET, a long distance telephone carrier. He holds a bachelor of science and a master's degree in mechanical engineering with a major in propulsion from Purdue University.

*Colonel Pollard and Joan Pollard on the high cliffs overlooking Lake Tahoe in August 2004.* Photo courtesy of Colonel Pollard.

*Colonel Pollard's homecoming to Colorado Springs on March 10, 1973. Having just flown in from the hospital in Wichita Falls, Texas, he went straight to his daughter Ginny's grade school to surprise her. The Pollard family walked up to the school on a cold March day and students, teachers, and families welcomed Colonel Pollard home after 2,120 days as a prisoner of war.* Photo courtesy of Colonel Pollard.

# Robinson Risner

*Military Rank:* Brigadier General, USAF (Ret.)

*Age When Captured:* 39

*Total Number of Days Held in Captivity in Vietnam:* 2,706

*Military Citations/Awards:* More than sixty-five awards and decorations, including two Air Force Crosses, Distinguished Service Medal, two Silver Stars, three Distinguished Flying Crosses, three Bronze Stars with "V" for Valor, four Purple Heart medals, eight Air Medals, and POW Medal.

The twentieth American jet ace, Brigadier General Risner earned this title before Vietnam by shooting down eight enemy aircraft during more than one hundred combat missions in Korea.

He has been inducted into both the Oklahoma Hall of Fame and the Oklahoma Air and Space Museum. In addition, he has received the Oklahoma Cross of Valor medal, as well as an honorary doctorate of law degree from the Oklahoma Christian College.

In 1979, General Risner became the first living person to be honored with the designation of a major military trophy in his name. Models of the Risner Trophy are presented to the outstanding Air Force fighter pilot each year.

*Residence:* San Antonio, Texas

*Current Occupation:* Retired

*Marital Status:* Married to Dorothy "Dot" Marie Risner

*Children:* 8

*Grandchildren:* 14

*Lt. Col. Robinson Risner, 40, as a prisoner of war in North Vietnam, 1965.* Photo courtesy of the Department of Defense.

# Biography:

After Vietnam, Brigadier General Risner was assigned to the 1st Tactical Fighter Wing at MacDill Air Force Base in Florida, served as the commander of the 832nd Air Division, and finished out his military career with a final assignment as the vice commander of the Fighter Weapons Center at Nellis Air Force Base in Nevada.

At the urging of his good friend Ross Perot and the governor of Texas, Brigadier General Risner then went to work as the executive director of the Texas War on Drugs for seven years, guiding it to the position of a national model for drug prevention. In 1985, he was appointed by President Reagan to serve as a U.S. Representative to the fortieth session of the United Nations General Assembly. He and his wife Dot are now retired in San Antonio. He has given many speeches on God and country, leadership, survival, and family values. He is the author of *The Passing of the Night,* a memoir about his POW experience.

In 2001, a nine-foot statue of Brigadier General Risner commissioned by Ross Perot was dedicated at the U.S. Air Force Academy. Its size is significant: as a captive, when Brigadier General Risner was released from solitary confinement, he organized a church service for his fellow POWs. This was against the prison rules, and he was severely beaten. As he was led away to punishment, the forty-six men remaining in the room spontaneously began singing the *Star Spangled Banner.* Asked how he felt when he heard the singing, he said, "I felt like I was nine feet tall and could go bear hunting with a switch." Two other statues of him have been erected at the U.S. Air Force Fighter Weapons Center and at Randolph Air Force Base.

*Brigadier General Risner at the White House with President Richard Nixon in 1973 soon after his return home. Risner is presenting the president with his book* The Passing of the Night. Photo courtesy of Brigadier General Risner.

# Wesley D. Schierman

*Military Rank:* Major, USAF (Ret.)

*Age When Captured:* 30

*Total Number of Days Held in Captivity in Vietnam:* 2,725

*Military Citations/Awards:* Silver Star Medal with two oak leaf clusters, Legion of Merit, Bronze Star with combat "V" and two oak leaf clusters, Purple Heart with oak leaf cluster, Air Medal with oak leaf cluster, POW Medal, and Good Conduct Medal (plus other decorations)

*Residence:* Everett, Washington

*Current Occupation:* Retired

*Marital Status:* Married to Faye A. Schierman

*Children:* 3

*Grandchildren:* 3

*Capt. Schierman embracing his wife Faye upon his return from deployment to Saudia Arabia in December 1963. Photo courtesy of the Canon Air Force Base, New Mexico.*

# Biography:

After returning from Vietnam, Major Schierman elected to resign from active duty and return to his former employment as an airline pilot for Northwest Airlines, where he flew as a captain on the B-727, DC-10, and B-747. He retired from Northwest in 1995.

Major Schierman holds a bachelor of science degree in psychology from Washington State University.

As one of two founding members of the "Blackjack Squadron," a formation-flying group of experimental airplanes, he initially trained twenty-nine current members of the squadron who fly up to sixteen experimental aircraft in close formation for air shows, fly-ins, memorial services, and various holidays.

*First Lieutenant Schierman seated in his*
*Washington Air National Guard F-89J at*
*Geiger Field in Spokane, Washington, 1959.*
Photo courtesy of Department of Defense.

*Three generations of the Schierman*
*family, Christmas 2003. Left to right:*
*Wendy, Alexa, Stacy, grandson Steven,*
*Steven, granddaughter Cassandra,*
*Sandra, Major Schierman, Faye.*
Photo courtesy of Major Schierman.

# Edwin A. Shuman III

*Military Rank:* Captain, USN (Ret.)

*Age When Captured:* 36

*Total Number of Days Held in Captivity in Vietnam:*
1,823

*Military Citations/Awards:* Silver Star, Legion of Merit
with combat "V," three Distinguished Flying Crosses,
two Bronze Stars with combat "V," two Purple Heart
medals, Air Medal, Navy Commendation Medal, and
POW Medal

In 2005, Captain Shuman was inducted into the Annapolis
Maritime Hall of Fame.

*Residence:* Annapolis, Maryland

*Current Occupation:* Retired

*Marital Status:* Married to Dona Horton Shuman

*Children:* 4

*Grandchildren:* 7

*Ensign Ned Shuman, 23, in
Pensacola, Florida, for flight
training, 1954.* Photo
courtesy of Captain Shuman.

# Biography:

After returning from Vietnam, Captain Shuman became the commanding
officer of VF-43 at Naval Air Station, Oceana. In addition, he served as the
commanding officer of Naval Station, Annapolis, and concurrently ran the U.S.
Naval Academy's sailing program from 1978 to 1982. His final military assignment took him to Bermuda as the officer in charge of the Naval Annex on the
island. He retired in 1984.

Since retirement, Captain Shuman has obtained numerous professional
licenses, including a private pilot's license, the Coast Guard one-hundred-ton
license, a glider's license, and a ham radio license. He surveyed boats and served

as a U.S. sailing measurer for twenty years. An avid yachtsman, he has twice won the Annapolis–Newport race (1991 and 1993) and came in third place in 1994 in the Newport–Bermuda race.

Captain Shuman keeps his Freedom 38 docked in his backyard in the winters and in Newport, Rhode Island, in the summers. He ferries himself between Annapolis and Newport in his RV-6. He has a bachelor's degree from the U.S. Naval Academy and worked on a master of business administration degree for one year at Old Dominion University.

*Ens. Nicholas Vanwagoner with his grandfather and USNA graduate Captain Shuman, at his graduation from the U.S. Naval Academy in May 2005.* Photo courtesy of David Vanwagoner.

*Christmas 1996 Shuman family photograph in their Annapolis, Maryland, home.* Photo courtesy of Captain Shuman.

# C. Everett Southwick

*Military Rank:* Captain, USN (Ret.)

*Age When Captured:* 35

*Total Number of Days Held in Captivity in Vietnam:* 2,122

*Military Citations/Awards:* Silver Star, Legion of Merit, Distinguished Flying Cross, Bronze Star, Purple Heart medals, Air Medals, and POW Medal

*Residence:* San Diego, California

*Current Occupation:* Retired

*Marital Status:* Divorced

*Children:* 4

*Grandchildren:* 5

*Cdr. Ev Southwick speaking in Lompoc, California, May 1973. Nancy Reagan was a guest at the event.* Photo courtesy of Captain Southwick.

# Biography:

Upon returning from Vietnam, Captain Southwick continued his military career in the Navy's Office of Legislative Affairs until his retirement in 1976. Following retirement, he served as director of congressional relations for two major international corporations, was appointed deputy assistant administrator for congressional relations at NASA, and was assistant for military and veterans affairs for San Diego Mayor Susan Golding and the Honorable Brian Bilbray.

Born in Fairbanks, Alaska, where his father was the head of the English and Foreign Languages Department at the University of Alaska, Fairbanks, Captain Southwick obtained a bachelor of arts degree from the University of Washington, where he was very active in his fraternity Alpha Delta Phi and where he first learned to play the ukulele. He earned a juris doctor degree from Hastings College of Law, University of California, San Francisco.

He is an avid golfer and takes an annual fishing trip to Alaska every summer with his son and a group of former POWs.

*Ev Southwick (on right) first learned to play the ukulele while a student at the University of Washington in the 1950s.* Photo courtesy of Captain Southwick.

*Captain Southwick returns to Vietnam. The man to the left of Southwick claims to be the son of the man who captured him and the man on the far left claims to be a witness to the shoot down and capture. Captain Southwick believes them both. This photograph was taken May 14, 2004, on the thirty-seventh anniversary of his shoot down.* Photo courtesy of Captain Southwick.

# James Bond Stockdale

*Military Rank:* Vice Admiral, USN (Ret.)

*Age When Captured:* 41

*Total Number of Days Held in Captivity in Vietnam:* 2,713

*Military Citations/Awards:* Twenty-six combat decorations including the Medal of Honor, three Distinguished Service Medals, four Silver Stars, two Distinguished Flying Crosses, two Purple Heart medals, and POW Medal

Vice Admiral Stockdale was the only three- or four-star officer in the history of the U.S. Navy to wear both aviator wings and the Medal of Honor.

In 1979, the Secretary of the Navy established the Vice Adm. James Bond Stockdale Leadership Award, which is presented annually to two commanding officers. In 1989, Monmouth College, in his native state of Illinois, named its student union the Stockdale Center. The following year he was made a 1990 Laureate of the Abraham Lincoln Academy of Illinois in ceremonies at the University of Chicago. In 1993, he was inducted into the Navy's Carrier Aviation Hall of Fame, and in 1995, he was inducted into the U.S. Naval Aviation Hall of Honor at the National Museum of Naval Aviation in Pensacola, Florida.

*Widow:* Sybil Bailey Stockdale resides in Coronado, California

*Children:* 4

*Grandchildren:* 8

*Ensign Stockdale and Sybil Bailey on their wedding day, June 28, 1947, at the Branford Congregational Church in Connecticut.* Photo courtesy of the Stockdale family.

# Biography:

After returning from Vietnam, Vice Admiral Stockdale served as president of the Naval War College in Newport, Rhode Island. He retired from the Navy in 1979 to become president of the Citadel, the military college of South Carolina. In 1981, he was named a senior research fellow with the Hoover Institution at Stanford University. He and his wife retired to Coronado, California, in a home which has been designated an historic landmark and renamed after them.

Vice Admiral Stockdale earned a bachelor of science degree from the U.S. Naval Academy, a master's degree from Stanford University, and eleven honorary doctoral degrees including a doctor of law degree from Brown University. He taught courses at the War College, Hampden-Sydney College, Stanford University, and other institutions. He served as Ross Perot's vice presidential running mate in 1992.

Vice Admiral Stockdale and his wife Sybil cowrote a best-selling book about their POW experience, *In Love and War*, which was made into an NBC television movie in 1987. He also published *A Vietnam Experience: Ten Years of Reflection*.

He died on July 5, 2005.

*Vice Admiral Stockdale with his four sons in February 1986. Left to right: Taylor, Stanford, Vice Admiral Stockdale, Sidney, Jimmy.* Photo courtesy of the Stockdale family.

*Lieutenant Colonel Risner and Commander Stockdale, the two most senior ranking POWs, in prison in Hanoi, exact date unknown.* Photo courtesy of the Department of Defense.

# Richard A. Stratton

*Military Rank:* Captain, USN (Ret.)

*Age When Captured:* 34

*Total Number of Days Held in Captivity in Vietnam:* 2,251

*Military Citations/Awards:* Silver Star, Legion of Merit, Bronze Star, Purple Heart medal, Air Medal, Navy Commendation Medal, Combat Action Ribbon, and POW Medal

*Residence:* Atlantic Beach, Florida

*Current Occupation:* Retired naval aviator

*Marital Status:* Married to Alice M. Robertson Stratton

*Children:* 3

*Grandchildren:* 6

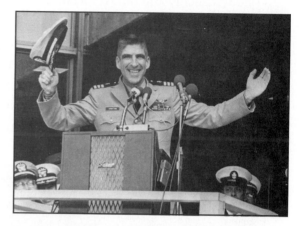

*Cdr. Richard A. Stratton, 41, has a smile for the crowd at Oak Knoll Naval Hospital in Oakland, California, as he arrives home on March 8, 1973. Commander Stratton was the first man off the plane.* Photo courtesy of Department of Defense.

# Biography:

After returning from Vietnam, Captain Stratton continued his military career, accumulating more than three thousand hours in jet aircraft and three hundred aircraft carrier landings. He is rated by the FAA as a commercial pilot. After retiring from the Navy, he was trained and commenced practice as a clinical social worker, specializing in the areas of psychological trauma and addictions. He served as chairman of the Veterans Affairs Advisory Committee on Prisoners of War and as president of the NAM-POWs organization.

Captain Stratton and his wife, also a clinical social worker and a former assistant secretary of the Navy for force support and families, retired from their social work practice in 2001. He is a member of the Board of Trustees for the Children's Crisis Center Inc., a member of the board of directors of Beaches Counseling Associates Inc., and a member/volunteer of the Jacksonville Beach Police Academy Alumni Association.

Captain Stratton holds a bachelor of arts degree in history and government from Georgetown University, a master of arts degree in international relations from Stanford University, and a master of social work from Rhode Island College School of Social Work. Two of his sons and a daughter-in-law are former Marines and combat veterans of Operation Desert Storm.

In 2005, the "A" team added a new member: baby Annaliese.

*The first family portrait taken upon Stratton's return home from Hanoi, North Vietnam, October 1973. Left to right: Charles, Alice, Pat, Captain Stratton, Mike.* Photo courtesy of Captain Stratton.

*The second annual Stratton family reunion at Camp Michigania in Boyne, Michigan, June 2004.* Photo courtesy of Captain Stratton.

# Orson G. Swindle III

*Military Rank:* Lieutenant Colonel, USMC (Ret.)

*Age When Captured:* 29

*Total Number of Days Held in Captivity in Vietnam:* 2,305

*Military Citations/Awards:* More than twenty military decorations for valor, including two Silver Stars, two Legions of Merit, two Bronze Stars, two Purple Heart medals, and POW Medal

Lieutenant Colonel Swindle has been recognized for his leadership in various professional capacities as the 2005 RSA Conference Award for Public Policy by the Cyber Security Industry Alliance, the 2004 Privacy Leadership Award by the International Association of Privacy Professionals, and the 2003 World War II Marine Raiders "Point Man" Award for his lifetime of leadership and "pointing the way."

*Residence:* Alexandria, Virginia

*Current Occupation:* former Federal Trade Commissioner (his term ended in June 2005); executive consultant

*Marital Status:* Married to Angela Williams

*Children:* 2

*Grandchildren:* None

*Capt. Orson Swindle flying with Squadron VMF (AW)-235 in Beaufort, South Carolina, 1965.* Photo courtesy of the Department of Defense.

# Biography:

Upon returning from Vietnam, Lieutenant Colonel Swindle finished out his military career and served in the Reagan administration as assistant secretary of commerce and the Georgia State director of the Farmers Home Administration for the Department of Agriculture. He served as the national spokesperson for Ross Perot during his 1992 presidential campaign, becoming the first national leader of United We Stand America.

He worked with former cabinet secretaries Jack Kemp and William Bennett, former Congressman Vin Weber, and Ambassador Jeanne Kirkpatrick to form Empower America. In 1994 and 1996, he was the Republican candidate for Congress in Hawaii's first congressional district.

Lieutenant Colonel Swindle served as a federal trade commissioner from 1997 to 2005 and is now an advisor on public policy isues concerning information and privacy. He holds a bachelor of science degree in industrial management from Georgia Tech and a master of business administration from Florida State University. He is a frequent public speaker on public policy, particularly on the topics of information system security and privacy, as well as on motivation, overcoming adversities, and executive leadership.

*Maj. Jim Harrison, Maj. Orson Swindle, and Maj. Joe Lavin at the Naval Hospital in Jacksonville, Florida, on March 7, 1973, the night Major Swindle returned home.* Photo courtesy of Commissioner Swindle.

*Commissioner Swindle and his wife Angie on New Year's Eve 2004.* Photo courtesy of Commissioner Swindle.

# Who Are the
# Vietnam-Era POWs?

O f the 802 prisoners of war held in Southeast Asia (661 military, 141 civilians/ foreign nationals), 472 were imprisoned in North Vietnam—some for longer than eight years. In South Vietnam, 266 were held in jungle POW camps—one for as long as nine years. Of the remainder, 28 were in Laos, 31 in Cambodia, and 5 in China.[1]

Following repatriation in early 1973, the returnees formed what is now one of the strongest fraternal organizations that exist in the world today. They are bonded together, not by rank or service, but by the deep knowledge and faith that they survived—together—as the longest-held group of POWs in our nation's history.

Who are they? Where are they? What are they doing with their lives today? How is their health—physically and mentally? How do they as a group compare demographically and historically to other wars' POWs thirty years later? Take a look at some of the statistics of the 661 military POWs who returned home.

## How many POWs were held in Southeast Asia?

Considering this protracted war ended the lives of 58,200 men and women of our armed forces, it is surprising to realize that only 725 uniformed U.S. servicemen are known to have been captured alive.[2] (By comparison, in the four years of World War II, more than 130,200 U.S. servicemen were captured alive.)

However, information gleaned from eyewitness accounts told by the American POWs returned to U.S. control confirms that 725 military POWs were alive while in Vietnamese control. Sixty-four of those died at the hands of their captors: 2 died in Cambodian camps, 3 died in Laotian camps, 23 died in prisons in North Vietnam, and 36 died in primitive camps in South Vietnam. Most of those who died in South Vietnamese camps were enlisted men who were beaten, denied medical treatment, or executed. Most of those who died in North Vietnam were air crew (22 officers and 1 warrant officer) who died as a result of torture or poor medical treatment.

# Facts about the 661 survivors, by service and location held

There were 139 Army POWs, 333 Air Force POWs, 38 Marine POWs, and 151 Navy POWs who returned home alive following our nation's involvement in Vietnam (July 8, 1959, to May 15, 1975). Of those:

- 23 were held in Cambodia—none escaped
  17 Army enlisted men, 1 Air Force officer, and 5 Navy enlisted men
- 2 were held in China—neither escaped
  1 Air Force pilot, 1 Navy pilot
- 15 were held in Laos—2 Navy pilots escaped
  3 Army (1 pilot, 1 military attaché, and 1 enlisted man), 7 Air Force pilots, 1 enlisted Marine air crewman, and 4 Navy (3 pilots and 1 enlisted sailor)
- 468 were in held North Vietnam—none escaped
  319 Air Force pilots or air crewmen, 9 Marine aviators, and 140 Navy (139 aviation officers and one enlisted sailor)
- 158 were held in South Vietnam—17 Army, 1 Air Force, and 10 Marines escaped
  123 Army (30 pilots, 13 air crew, and 80 ground troops), 6 Air Force (5 pilots and 1 civil engineer), 28 Marines (5 pilots and 23 ground troops), and 1 Navy pilot

In the entire Vietnam War, there were only 30 successful escapes (2 from Laos, 28 from South Vietnam). There were dozens of thwarted escape attempts in South Vietnam and 17 military men who tried multiple escapes in North Vietnam—all unsuccessful.

# The first, the last, and the longest

- The first military POW was Army Maj. Lawrence R. Bailey Jr. Major Bailey was the military attaché serving in the U.S. Embassy, Vientiane, Laos. He was a passenger in a C-47 that was shot down on March 23, 1961 in Laos. He was released on August 15, 1962. The two-man crew and five other military passengers all perished. They are listed by Department of Defense as the first military men killed in the Vietnam War.
- The first POW held in South Vietnam was Army Cpl. George Fryett. He was a classified publications clerk in Saigon when captured December 24, 1961. He was released June 24, 1962.

- The first POW captured in North Vietnam was Lt. (j.g.) Everett Alvarez Jr. Lieutenant Alvarez was shot down while flying an A-4C Skyhawk from the USS *Constellation* on August 5, 1964, during the first raids of the Gulf of Tonkin Incident. He was released February 12, 1973.
- Two pilots were downed by Chinese fighters when they strayed over Chinese territory. Air Force Capt. Phillip E. Smith was shot down in his F-104C on September 20, 1965. He was kept in solitary confinement in Peking, China, for more than seven years. Navy Lt. Robert J. Flynn was shot down in his A-6A on August 21, 1967, and was also kept in solitary confinement in China. Both were released on March 15, 1973.
- The first POWs captured in Cambodia were Army Cpl. Ronald J. Lehrman Army PFC Jerry A. Tester. They were captured while driving a patrol boat on a Cambodian river on May 20, 1968. They were released June 10, 1968.
- The longest-held POW in South Vietnam—and during the Vietnam War—was Army Capt. Floyd J. Thompson. Captain Thompson was a Special Forces advisor to the Vietnamese army. He was held as a POW for al most nine years from March 26, 1964, until March 16, 1973. He is thought to be the longest-held military POW in the history of U.S. warfare.
- The last military POW captured was Navy Lt. Cdr. Phillip A. Kientzler. He was shot down just south of the demilitarized zone on January 27, 1973. He was flying what was probably the last combat mission of the Vietnam War. He was captured the same day the peace accords were being signed halfway around the world in Paris. He was released on March 27, 1973.
- The last military POW to be released was Army Capt. Robert T. White. He was captured in South Vietnam on November 11, 1969. He was held in solitary confinement in a bamboo cage for more than three years. Captain White was not released until April 1, 1973, in violation of the Paris Peace Accords which specified that all POWs would be exchanged by March 31, 1973.

## Why were the majority of the Vietnam POWs commissioned officers, and why were most of them aviators?

In previous wars, the vast majority of prisoners of war were enlisted personnel. The Vietnam War was unusual in that there were more officers captured (approximately 78 percent) than enlisted (approximately 22 percent). This is mainly because the four services committed significant air power to interdicting lines of communication between North Vietnam and South Vietnam, supporting ground operations and attacking airfields in North Vietnam. Of the 661 military POWs, 143 were enlisted, 504 were commissioned officers, and 14 were warrant officers.

Most of the missions in North Vietnam were completed by aviators from the Air Force, Navy, and Marines. Being an aviator during the Vietnam War required some college and an officer's commission. Most of the pilots held a college degree. The missions these aviators were asked to perform were very dangerous and thousands of aircraft were lost. Untold hundreds of helicopters were shot down or lost; the actual totals are unavailable. However, records exist for the number of fixed wing aircraft shot down during the Vietnam War:

- Air Force: 2,197 aircraft lost, 2,449 fatalities, 341 POWs
- Navy: 854 aircraft lost, 575 fatalities, 144 POWs
- Marines: 271 aircraft lost, 241 fatalities, 12 POWs[3]

The Army used a great number of warrant officers as pilots, but most served in helicopters. Most of the downed Army helicopter air crews were not listed as MIAs or POWs because either they were rescued or their bodies were recovered.

## What were the demographics of the POWs?

The race and ethnicity of those who served in Vietnam has been hotly debated over the years. Many press reports indicated that the war was fought by a large number of poor minorities, disproportionate to their percentage of the U.S. population. The actual statistics show a different picture. Of the combat casualties in Vietnam, 86 percent of the service members were Caucasians, 12.5 percent were African-American, and 1.2 percent of them were of other racial or ethnic descent.[4]

Sociologists Charles C. Moskos and John Sibley Butler, in their recently published book *All That We Can Be*, analyzed the claim that blacks were used like cannon fodder during Vietnam "and can report definitely that this charge is untrue. Black fatalities amounted to 12 percent of all Americans killed in Southeast Asia—a figure proportional to the number of blacks in the U.S. population at the time and slightly lower than the proportion of blacks in the Army at the close of the war."[5] As for the Vietnam War POW population, 630 (95 percent) were Caucasian (includes Philipino and Hispanic descent), 27 (4 percent) were Negroid (Black), and 4 (1 percent) were of Mongoloid (Asian) descent.

## POWs of Distinction

The POWs from the Vietnam War were a stubborn cadre of fighters and, for the most part, they strictly abided by the U.S. Code of Conduct and resisted their captors, for better or for worse. Many of them paid dearly for it, physically and emotionally. In recognition of their resistance, bravery, and heroism, a total of eight POWs from the Vietnam conflict received the Congressional Medal of Honor, our country's highest decoration.[6]

The NAM-POWs organization has three living Medal of Honor recipients in their ranks:

- Sgt. Maj. Jon Robert Cavaiani, USA (Ret.)
- Col. George Everette "Bud" Day, USAF (Ret.)
- Col. Leo Keith Thorsness, USAF (Ret.)

Medal of Honor recipient Vice Adm. James Bond Stockdale, USN (Ret.), died in July 2005.

Four other POWs received the Medal of Honor posthumously:

- Col. Donald G. Cook, USMC
- PFC William D. Port, USA
- Capt. Lance P. Sijan, USAF
- Capt. Humbert Roque "Rocky" Versace, USA

## How many of the Vietnam POWs served in other armed conflicts?

Many of the Vietnam POWs also served their country by fighting in other armed conflicts, either prior to or subsequent to their prolonged captivity in Vietnam.

*Vietnam POWs who served in World War II:* 2d Lt. James E. Bean, USA Air Corps; Cpl. George "Bud" Day, USMC; 1st Lt. John Peter Flynn, USA Air Corps; Pvt. John W. Frederick, USMC; 2d Lt. Norman C. Gaddis, USA Air Corps, served but not in combat; 2d Lt. Lawrence N. Guarino, USA Air Corps; 2d Lt. Laird Guttersen, USA Air Corps, served in a B-25 pilot pool but did not fly missions; PO1 Harry T. Jenkins, USN; Sgt. James H. Kasler, USA Air Corps; 2d Lt. Richard P. "Pop" Keirn, USA Air Corps; Flight Cadet Gordon A. Larson and Flight Cadet Konrad W. Trautman were seventeen-year-old aviation cadets in the USA Air Corps when World War II ended; 1st Lt. Vernon P. Ligon, USA Air Corps; 2d Lt. Robbie Risner, U.S. Army Air Force; Pvt. Kenneth A. Simonet, USMC; 2d Lt. Harvey S. Stockman, USA Air Corps; and SN Richard F. Williams, U.S. Merchant Marines.

*Vietnam POWs who served in Korea:* Cpl. Richard E. Bolstad, USMC; 2d Lt. Ernest C. Brace, USMC; 1st Lt. Ronald E. Byrne, USAF; 1st Lt. Fred V. Cherry, USAF; Ens. Verlyne W. Daniels, USN; 1st Lt. George "Bud" Day, USAF; 1st Lt. Richard A. Dutton, USAF; 1st Lt. John Peter Flynn, USAF; GySgt. John W. Frederick, USMC; Capt. Norman C. Gaddis, USAF; AN2 James W. Gough, USAF; Capt. Lawrence N. Guarino, USAF; 2d Lt. Laird Guttersen, USAF; 1st Lt. Theodore W. Guy, USAF; Lt. (j.g.) Harry T. Jenkins; 2d Lt. Samuel R. Johnson, USAF; 1st Lt. James H. Kasler, USAF; 1st Lt. Thomas H. Kirk, USAF; 2d Lt. James L. Lamar, USAF; 1st Lt. Raymond J. Merritt, USAF; Lt. (j.g.) Leo T. Profilet, USN; 1st Lt. Benjamin H. Purcell, USA; Capt. Robinson Risner, USAF; Ens. Wendell B. Rivers, USN; PO1 David J. Rollins, USN; Ens. Howard E. Rutledge, USN; 1st Lt. Thomas J. Sterling, USAF; 1st Lt. Konrad W. Trautman, USAF; Capt. Richard F. Williams, USA; and Lt. (j.g.) Robert D. Woods, USN.

*Vietnam POW who served in Chile-Peru border conflict (1975):* CWO3 David W. Sooter, USA, was killed flying for the CIA as an observer during the Peru–Ecuador border wars in 1975.

*Vietnam POWs who served in Desert Storm (1991):* Col. David E. Baker, USAF; Lt. Col. Richard C. Brenneman, USAF; Col. William G. Byrns, USAF; Lt. Col. Thomas J. Hanton, USAF; Col. James D. Kula, USAF; Capt. Thomas

B. Latendresse, USN; Col. Richard H. McDow, USAF; and Vice Adm. Joseph S. Mobley, USN, who was Commander, Naval Air Forces, Atlantic, at the time.

*Vietnam POW who served in Urgent Fury (Grenada):* Maj. Richard C. Anshus, USA, was the seventh man on the ground for the U.S.-led invasion to rescue American students.

*Vietnam POWs who served in the War on Terrorism:* Maj. Gen. Ed Mechenbier, USAF, was Mobilization Assistant to the Commander AFMC/CR DSN 787-4227. As the "last man standing"—the last NAM-POW still in uniform, Major General Mechenbier flew the "Hanoi Taxi" to Hanoi in June 2004 to bring back repatriated MIA remains. This was one of the last missions flown by that particular C-141, the plane that earned its nickname from Operation Homecoming. The Hanoi Taxi flew repeated missions to Hanoi to bring the POWs home in February and March 1973. The Hanoi Taxi will be officially retired in 2006 during the NAM-POWs' annual reunion in Dayton, Ohio. Major General Mechenbier retired in 2004.

Col. Charlie Brown, USAFR, was stationed at Westover ARB MA and was assigned as the 439 Airlift Wing Logistics Group Commander. Colonel Brown also retired in 2004.

## How many of the Vietnam POWs have pursued appointed or elected office?

This group has a high number of individuals who pursued post-military careers in public service. Many of them have commented that they became minor celebrities upon their return from Vietnam, which helped to catapult them into the public eye. As one of the few bright spots of the war, the release and return of our Vietnam POWs was highly celebrated, unlike the return of most Vietnam veterans, who came home without public recognition and quietly blended back into society. The returning POWs were treated to a White House dinner, invited to speak at numerous national and local events, and given many homecoming parades. Here are a few who continued to serve in appointed or elected public office:

- The Honorable Everett Alvarez Jr., Cdr., USN (Ret.)—Served as deputy director of the Peace Corps (1981–1982), deputy administrator of the Veterans Administration (1982–1986), and advisor/commissioner to four presidents
- The Honorable Larry Chesley, Lt. Col., USAF (Ret.)—Served as state senator from Arizona (1995–2001)
- The Honorable Tom Collins, Lt. Col., USAF (Ret.)—Served as assistant secretary of labor in the first Bush administration and ran as Republican nominee for Congress from the fourth district of Mississippi (1988)
- The Honorable Jeremiah Denton, Rear Adm., USN (Ret.)—Served as U.S. senator from Alabama (1980–1986)
- The Honorable Markham Gartley—Served as secretary of state of Maine (1975–1978)
- The Honorable Sam Johnson, Col., USAF (Ret.)—Serving as U.S. Congressman from Texas (1991 to present)
- The Honorable Joe Kernan—Served as lieutenant governor and governor from the State of Indiana (2001–2004)
- The Honorable John McCain, Capt., USN (Ret.)—Serving as U.S. senator from the State of Arizona (1987 to present), served as U.S. congressman from the State of Arizona (1982–1987), and as presidential candidate in 2000
- The Honorable Harry Monlux, Col., USAF (Ret.) (deceased)—Served in the Oklahoma House of Representatives (1975–1980)
- The Honorable Douglas Peterson, Col., USAF (Ret.)—Served as three-term U.S. congressman from Florida (1991–1996), and served as the first U.S. ambassador to the Socialist Republic of Vietnam (1998–2001), after normalization of diplomatic relations during the Clinton presidency
- The Honorable Benjamin H. Purcell, Col., USA (Ret.)—Served in the Georgia State Legislature (1995–1996)
- James Shively—Served as the assistant U.S. attorney, eastern district of Washington (1984–2000) and as the U.S. attorney, eastern district of Washington (2000–2001)
- Capt. C. Everett Southwick, USN (Ret.)—Served as deputy assistant

administrator for congressional relations at NASA (1987–1993)

- Vice Adm. James B. Stockdale, USN (Ret.)—Ran as the vice presidential candidate on the ticket with Ross Perot in 1992
- The Honorable Orson G. Swindle III, Lt. Col., USMC (Ret.)—Served as assistant secretary of commerce (1985–1989), ran as a Republican congressional candidate from Hawaii (1994 and 1996), and federal trade commissioner (1997–2005)
- The Honorable Leo Keith Thorsness, Col., USAFG (Ret.)—Served as state senator from Washington (1988–1992). He was narrowly defeated in a senatorial race with incumbent U.S. Senator George McGovern in 1974 and was narrowly defeated by Tom Daschle in a 1978 South Dakota congressional race—by a margin of only fourteen votes
- The Honorable James Warner—Served as domestic policy advisor to President Reagan (1981–1989)
- The Honorable Ronald Webb, Col., USAF (Ret.)—Served as special assistant to the administrator of the Federal Aviation Administration (1988– 1999), as special assistant to the secretary of transportation (1989)

## How many servicemen and -women are still unaccounted for—or MIA—from Vietnam?

There are 1,835 military casualties still unaccounted for from the Vietnam War.[7] By comparison, approximately 80,000 are MIA from World War II and some 8,200 are still MIA from the Korean War (1950–1953).

## Were there any female POWs in Vietnam?

No military servicewomen were captured. However, a handful of civilian women were captured and held as prisoners in Vietnam. Dr. Marjorie Nelson, a Quaker affiliated with International Voluntary Services (IVS), and Sandra Johnson, a teacher, also with IVS, were captured in Hue on February 5, 1968, and were both released on March 31, 1968.

Monika Schwinn, a West German volunteer nurse, was the only survivor of a group of five nurses (two male and three female) captured and held in South Vietnam. They were working for an aid organization called the Knights of Malta.

Schwinn was captured on April 27, 1969, and was force-marched to Hanoi, a distance of several hundred miles. She was kept in solitary confinement for almost four years. She was released on March 5, 1973, and flew to the United States on the same plane with the released military POWs. She still works in the medical field in her native Germany.

In addition, there were two missionaries who were captured and died in captivity: Dr. Eleanor Vietti, captured in 1962, and Betty Ann Olsen, captured on February 1, 1968. They both served with the Christian and Missionary Alliance (CMA) group in Ban Me Thuot, Darlac Province, in the Central Highlands of South Vietnam. They lived at CMA's compound, and they worked with the Montagnards, the Malayo-Polynesian and Mon-Khmer ethnic minorities who live in the mountains of Vietnam.

## Were the Vietnam POWs promoted after repatriation?

Following repatriation of the POWs, all services afforded their POWs the opportunity to continue with their military careers, unless they were deemed medically disabled. During their incarceration, the POWs were promoted to higher ranks along with their contemporaries. In fact, some returned home to discover they were two ranks higher than when they were captured.

## How many Vietnam POWs remained in the military, and how many became admirals and generals?

Approximately 80 percent of the returning POWs remained in the military until they were eligible for retirement (twenty years). Twenty-four Vietnam POWs attained the rank of admiral or general:

**4-Star** (O-10): Gen. Charles G. Boyd, USAF (Ret.)

**3-Star** (O-9): Lt. Gen. John P. Flynn, USAF (Ret.) (deceased), Vice Adm. William P. Lawrence, USN (Ret.), Vice Adm. Edward H. Martin, USN (Ret.), Vice Adm. Joseph S. Mobley, USN (Ret.), and Vice Adm. James B. Stockdale, USN (Ret.) (deceased)

**2-Star** (O-8): Maj. Gen. John L. Borling, USAF (Ret.), Maj. Gen. William J. Breckner, USAF (Ret.), Rear Adm. Jeremiah E. Denton, USN (Ret.), Rear Adm. Robert Byron Fuller, USN (Ret.), Maj. Gen. Edward J. Mechenbier, USAF

(Ret.), and Rear Adm. Robert H. Shumaker, USN (Ret.)

**1-Star** (O-7): Brig. Gen. David E. Baker, USAF (Ret.), Brig. Gen. Ralph T. Browning, USAF (Ret.), Brig. Gen. Jeffrey T. Ellis, USAF (Ret.), Brig. Gen. Kenneth R. Fleenor, USAF (Ret.), Brig. Gen. Norman C. Gaddis, USAF (Ret.), Brig. Gen. James D. Latham, USAF (Ret.), Brig. Gen. Alan P. Lurie, USAF (Ret.), Brig. Gen. Kenneth W. North, USAF (Ret.), Brig. Gen. Jon A. Reynolds, USAF (Ret.), Brig. Gen. Robinson Risner, USAF (Ret.), Brig. Gen. James E. Sehorn, USAF (Ret.), and Brig. Gen. David W. Winn, USAF (Ret.)

## What kinds of professions did the Vietnam POWs pursue after returning (after finishing their military careers)? What kinds of professional degrees did they pursue?

While statistics are not kept on the subsequent professions the POWs pursued upon their return and after retiring from the military, anecdotal evidence of their varied professions and avocations includes a roster of doctors, lawyers, authors, politicians, corporate executives, veterinarians, small business owners, ambassadors, commissioners, ministers, psychologists, commercial airline pilots, real estate agents/brokers, computer consultants, teachers and professors, athletic coaches, artists, home builders, community volunteers, church elders, philanthropists, public speakers, world travelers—and, of course, fathers and grandfathers.

## Have the POWs published any books on their experience?

More than thirty-five books have been penned and published by the former POWs on their respective POW experiences and on other academic and leadership subjects. A list of these books can be found on the POWs' website: www.nampows.org.

## How many Vietnam POWs suffer from post-traumatic stress disorder (PTSD)? How do their rates of PTSD

## compare with the average Vietnam veteran and with POWs from other conflicts?

The Robert E. Mitchell Center for Prisoner of War Studies, located at the Naval Air Station in Pensacola, Florida, provides follow-up studies of repatriated prisoners of war as a result of World War II and the Korea, Vietnam, Desert Storm, and Operation Iraqi Freedom conflicts. The studies document whether the POWs have captivity-related physical or mental problems. This information is gathered in the context of extensive annual evaluations, the results of which are released to the patient for routine health maintenance. Additionally, the information gathered is used in support of real-world operations.

For example, the center reported results of extensive studies performed on seventy Navy POWs from Vietnam and compared them to fifty-five naval aviators of approximately the same age and rank. These two groups were assessed on an annual basis for more than two decades. "Twenty years following repatriation, the former Navy aviator POWs reported more physical health problems [as compared to the control group of Vietnam-era Navy aviators who did not experience captivity]. . . . Interestingly, mental health problems were relatively infrequent among this sample of repatriated POWs, and rates of PTSD and adjustment problems did not differ from the comparison sample (Nice et al., 1996)."

"The cumulative incidence rates of 4 percent for PTSD and 14 percent for adjustment disorders among the repatriated Navy POWs is consistent with lifetime prevalence rates in community-based samples (American Psychiatric Association, 1994) and much lower than the lifetime prevalence rates of 30.6 percent for PTSD and 44.5 percent for serious postwar readjustment problems in the sample of male Vietnam theater veterans in the NVVRS, a more demographically diverse group than the present sample (Kulka et al., 1990)."[8]

## Why don't the POWs exhibit higher rates of PTSD—given that they were held captive for so long, deprived of so much, and treated so inhumanely?

Several studies have pointed to the POWs' higher age and education levels as indicative of their resiliency. An informal poll of 300 of the POWs in 1971 (those incarcerated in North Vietnam) determined that the average age of the air crews was thirty-three years old, their average education level was four or more years of college, and their average rank was 0-4 (major or lieutenant commander).[9] Within the group of POWs, the strongest resisters to some of the most abusive treatment were identified as older, more senior in rank, more outgoing and extroverted, and more energetic.[10]

In other words, the higher age and maturity level of the Vietnam POWs apparently gave them a psychological "buffer" that the average Vietnam veterans did not have. By comparison, the average age of the U.S. Vietnam serviceman was about nineteen years old and his education level average was twelfth grade.[11]

## Do the Vietnam POWs suffer from any long-term or chronic physical ailments or pain from their experience in Vietnam?

Many of the POWs from Vietnam tolerate chronic pain and a range of disabilities—from minor to major—caused by their capture (involving violent, high-speed ejections from aircraft and jolting parachute landings), torture, poor nutrition, and inadequate medical attention during the many years of their captivity. Studies have shown that, as a group, the POWs suffer from higher incidences of chronic disorders of the peripheral nervous system, joints, and back—when compared to the control group.[12]

## Is the divorce rate of Vietnam POWs significantly higher than that of their military (non-POW) counterparts of the same age?

This question is commonly asked and hard to answer. When the group of Navy POWs was tracked against the Navy aviator control group, the POWs' divorce rate was much higher during the initial two years after repatriation— approximately twice that of the control group's divorce rate. Interestingly enough, the control group's divorce rate paralleled that of the POWs' divorce rate after 1975. Odds of remarriage were also very similar, but the incidence of subsequent divorces (two or three) is much higher among the Vietnam POWs. In general, the POWs had a higher likelihood of divorcing after repatriation if they were younger, had marriages of shorter duration, or if their wives were less satisfied with the marriage.[13]

A recent, informal poll conducted online by the Vietnam POWs yielded a statistical tie between those former POWs who were still married to their first wives and those who were divorced (many of whom have since remarried). Out of an existing 661 former POWs, 301 (46 percent) responded to the poll. Of these 301, 121 were divorced from the wife they were married to at the time of capture (46 percent), 140 were still married to the same wife (53 percent), and 40 were not married at the time of capture.[14]

There are many other variables that contributed to these statistics, such as length of captivity, duration of marriage prior to capture, age of both spouses, marital satisfaction prior to capture, maturity levels of both spouses, and the presence or absence of children.[15] All of the POWs will admit that their POW experience was stressful on their marriages and families. Some of the marriages fell apart as a result. But some relationships grew even stronger from the experience.

## Do they keep in touch with each other?

NAM-POWs Inc. is a nonprofit 501 (c) (19) veterans organization chartered by the State of Arizona in 1973. NAM-POWs came into existence through a need of the 802 returning prisoners of war (661 military and 141 captured civilians) repatriated from the Southeast Asia conflict to organize in such a way that they could continue to build upon their bonds of friendship and camaraderie developed during captivity.

NAM-POWs is dedicated to the principles of patriotic allegiance to the United States, fidelity to its Constitution and laws, the security of civil liberty, and the perpetuation of free institutions. Its objectives are to cherish the memories of the valiant deeds of their members, promote true fellowship among their members, advance the best interests of members of the Armed Forces of the United States, enhance their prestige and understanding by example and personal activity, and stimulate patriotism and national pride in the minds of their youth.

They gather for social reunions every year, much like many other fraternal or educational organizations. They bring their spouses, children, siblings, grandchildren, and friends. They raise money for charitable causes. They keep in touch on vacation together, on the phone and via email—and they can still remember the tap code they developed and used to communicate with each other behind bars and between walls. They are family to each other.

For more information on the NAM-POWs, visit their web site at www.nampows.org.

## Notes

1. This fact and many others cited in this section were gleaned from "Mac's Facts." Collected by Capt. Michael McGrath, USN (Ret.), former POW and former president of the NAM-POWs Corp., this compendium of statistics on the Vietnam POWs was collected because Captain McGrath has fielded numerous questions for more than thirty years from news organizations, researchers, other POWs, and MIA families. The numerical statistics he has assembled are obtained from the Defense Prisoner of War/Missing Personnel Office (DPMO) Reference Document, U.S. Personnel Missing, Southeast Asia (and Selected Foreign Nationals) (PMSEA), December 2003. These statistics are also available online at: http://www.dtic.mil/dpmopmsea/files.htm. Captain McGrath has saved all his research and has graciously shared it for publication in this book. For more information on Mac's Facts, go to www.nampows.org.

2. Approximately 141 civilians and foreign nationals were captured in Southeast Asia during our nation's involvement in Vietnam. Some were CIA agents, some were contractors, some were aid workers, and some were tourists. As the focus of this book is the uniformed service personnel who were held as POWs, the civilian prisoners are not included.

3. Chris Hobson, *Vietnam Air Losses, United States Air Force, Navy and Marine Corps Fixed Wing Aircraft Losses in Southeast Asia 1961–1973* (Hinckley, Eng.: Midland Publishing, 2000), 268. Hobson includes those fixed wing pilots who died in prison camps; so the totals will not equal the fixed wing pilots who got out alive in 1973.

4. B. G. Burkett and Glenna Whitley, *Stolen Valor* (Dallas, TX: Verity Press, 1998), 454.

5. Charles C. Moskos and John Sibley Butler, *All That We Can Be: Black Leadership and Racial Integration the Army Way* (New York: Basic Books, 1996), 8.

6. For a comprehensive and intimate look at 117 Medal of Honor recipients, see *Medal of Honor: Portraits of Valor Beyond the Call of Duty,* photographed and written by Nick Del Cazo and Peter Collier, respectively, and published by Artisan, 2003.

7. Robert E. Klein, PhD, Michael R. Wells, M.S., and Janet Somers, B.A., "Former American Prisoners of War (POWs)" (Washington, DC: U.S. Department of Veterans Affairs, April 2005), 6.

8. Catherine L. Cohan, Steven Cole, and Joanne Davila, *Risk and Resilience Following Repatriation: Marital Transitions Among Vietnam-Era Repatriated Prisoners of War* (Pennsylvania State University Population Research Institute, December 2003), 5. NVVRS was the National Vietnam Veterans Readjustment Study, a comprehensive study of a large sample of Vietnam veterans.

9. Captain McGrath provided the results of this informal, nonscientific poll taken among approximately 300 of the POWs incarcerated in North Vietnam in 1971.

10. Robert J. Ursano, MD, and Ann E. Norwood, MD, eds., *Emotional Aftermath of the Persian Gulf War* (Washington, DC: American Psychiatric Press, 1996), 455.

11. The Robert E. Mitchell Center for POW Studies.

12. Cohan et al., 5.

13. Cohan et al., 1 and 16.

14. Captain McGrath conducted this online poll in March and April 2005.

15. Cohan et al., 20.

## No Man Is an Island

No man is an island, entire of itself;
every man is a piece of the continent, a part of the main.
If a clod be washed away by the sea,
Europe is the less, as well as if a promontory were,
as well as if a manor of thy friend's or of thine own were.
Any man's death diminishes me, because I am involved in mankind;
and therefore never send to know for whom the bell tolls;
it tolls for thee.
—John Donne

# *Acknowledgments*

*J*amie Howren and Taylor Baldwin Kiland, the creators of *Open Doors: Vietnam POWs Thirty Years Later,* would like to recognize the following companies, foundations, and individuals who provided financial support, personal time, and tireless encouragement to us and to our vision. Without you, we would not have accomplished this dream. Thank you.

4th Allied P.O.W. Wing and Capt. Mike McGrath, who contributed his artwork, creativity, research, time, and love to this exhibit and this book.

15th Air Wing, Hickam Air Force Base

A Better Type
Ace Beverage
Aerospace Industries Association
David Alberg
Michael Allen
The Allen Family Foundation
The Honorable and Mrs. Everett Alvarez, Jr.
American Beverage Association
The American Legion
Donya Archer
Army Heritage Center Foundation
Mr. Michael Ashford
Mrs. Pat Atkinson
Atlas Fine Art Services
Austal USA
Axiom/Conwal
Mr. Warren W. Ayres

Mr. and Mrs. James Bain
The Honorable William Ball, III
Helen Bartels

Barbara Haskett Battelle
Mr. Robert Barker
Eloise Baza
Miss Ellis Beardsley
Capt. Norm Bednarek, USN (Ret.)
Robert Bennett
Jessica Bernanke
Mrs. Judy Bernanke
Lt. Cdr. and Mrs. John Bernard
B.G. Berndorf
Mr. Albert Berry
Rear Adm. David Bill, USN (Ret.)
Paula Blankenship
The Boaz Trust
The Boeing Company
Booz Allen Hamilton
Mr. Peter Bos
USS *Boxer* (LHD-4)
Mr. and Mrs. J. Richard Breen
Mr. Jack Brennen
Mr. and Mrs. Patrick Brogan
Tom Brokaw and *NBC Nightly News*

Basha's
Mr. and Mrs. Tony Brush
M.G. Buchanan
The Honorable and Mrs. William C. Bunch, Jr.
Mr. and Mrs. Steven Burchianti
Mr. and Mrs. David M. Burke
Burke and Herbert Bank and Trust Company
Vice Adm. and Mrs. Edward Burkhalter

CACI International Inc. and Mr. Jack London
Mr. John Campbell
Mr. John Barkey and Ms. Juliette Cane
The Honorable and Mrs. Frank Carlucci
Scott Carr
Dr. Clarke Caywood
CENTEX Construction Company
CESSI Technologies Inc.
Mr. Barnabas Chen
The Honorable Richard B. Cheney
Stan Cherney
Capt. David Church, USN (Ret.)
Mr. and Mrs. Michael Cifrino
Rear Adm. Steve Clarey, USN (Ret.)
Capt. and Mrs. William G. Clautice
Cloud 9 Shuttle
Mrs. Shari Cohen
Cdr. and Mrs. George Coker
Commonwealth Consulting Corporation
Rich Conti
Martha Cooper
Barbara Conly
Coronado Historical Association
Mr. and Mrs. J. Creighton
Mr. and Mrs. James Crocker
Nancy Crozier

Mr. Bob Daniels
Cameron Davidson
Col. and Mrs. George E. Day
Scott de Carillo
Col. and Mrs. Alan De Fend

Mr. and Mrs. De Francia
Robert De LaGrave
Mr. and Mrs. Tom Dean
The Stephen Decatur House Museum
Digital Output
Mr. and Mrs. Steven Dokosky
Dos Geckos Musicians
H.C. Dupuis

The Honorable and Mrs. Gordon England
Capt. and Mrs. John C. Ensch
Mr. and Mrs. Brooks Ensign

FedEx
Capt. and Mrs. John Heaphy Fellowes
Nan Ferguson
Mr. and Mrs. David Fiske
Mr. and Mrs. Perry Floyd
Adm. and Mrs. Cathal Flynn
Freedoms Foundation of Valley Forge
Free Library of Philadelphia
Gayle Freeman
John Freeman
Capt. and Mrs. Peter Fullenwider

Cdr. and Mrs. Paul Galanti
Mr. and Mrs. James Gallagher
Joe Galloway
The Honorable H. Lawrence Garrett III
Capt. and Mrs. F. Reginald Gaylord
GHL Incorporated
Evelyn Gelles
General Motors Corporation
Mr. William Gibbons
Valerie Gibbons
Mr. and Mrs. John H. J. Giddings
Dean Loren Ghiglione
Cathy Jessup Glessing
Mr. and Mrs. Whitney Goit
Guam Chamber of Commerce
San Diego County

**169**

Mr. and Mrs. William D. Grant
Mr. and Mrs. John Griffiths
Mr. G. Christopher Griner

Dr. Bob Hain
Bruce Hall and Watkins Meegan and Drury
The Hanger Orthopedic Group Inc.
Mr. and Mrs. Jonathon Hardin
Scott Harmon
Mr. and Mrs. Douglas Harpel
Mrs. Betty Harrington
Dr. and Mrs. F.B. Harrington
Mr. John P. Harrington
A. Page Harrington
Shelia Harrison
Mr. and Mrs. James H. Haskett Jr.
Mr. John Hawkins
Lt. Megan P. Hayes, USNR
Lt. Col. Buzz Hefti, USMC (Ret.)
Mr. Doug Hegdahl
Mr. and Mrs. Peter Henry
Cdr. Lawrence Heyworth III, USN (Ret.)
Adm. J. R. Hogg, USN (Ret.)
Mrs. Joan G. Ogilvy Holden
Mr. and Mrs. Peter Horrigan
Mr. and Mrs. Melinda Curtis Howes
Mr. and Mrs. James H. Howren Jr.
Mr. and Mrs. James H. Howren Sr.
Mrs. Jo Haskett Howren
Huffman Press
Anthony Huggett and Karla Odeen
Mr. and Mrs. Peter Hughes
Mr. and Mrs. Frank O. Hunnewell
Capt. and Mrs. Duffy Hutton

Ice Simulations

Mr. and Mrs. Lee Janka
Capt. and Mrs. Wollom Jensen
Mr. and Mrs. Andrew Jessup
Carla Jones
Mr. Rod Johnston
Mr. and Mrs. Russell Kale

Mr. and Mrs. Michael Kaluza
Mr. and Mrs. Matthew Kambrod
Mr. and Mrs. John Kane
Mr. Steven Karalekas
Capt. and Mrs. Taylor Keith
Kate Keith
KenCom Graphic Design
Mr. Paul Kessel
Mr. and Mrs. Lee C. Kitchin
Capt. and Mrs. Ingolf N. Kiland Jr.
Mr. and Mrs. Ingolf N. Kiland III
Col. Fred Kiley, USAF (Ret.)
Rear Adm. Randolph W. King, USN (Ret.)
Mr. Norm Koenig and Mrs. Gwen
    Jensen Koenig
Ginger and Sergio Koloszyc
Diane Kresch
Capt. Lou Kriser, USN (Ret.)
Martin Kruming
Mr. Peter Kunkel
Col. Floyd Harold Kushner, MD,
    FACS, USA (Ret.)

Mr. and Mrs. John Leary
Mr. Christopher M. Lehman, Ph.D.
Mrs. Irve C. LeMoyne
Alan Lerchbacker
LITHO GRAPHICS, Randy Carr
Lowe Enterprises

Mr. and Mrs. Thomas MacMillan
Mr. and Mrs. Ross Mackenzie
Michael and Cindi Malinick
The Honorable Gordon Mansfield
Map Trust
Marines' Memorial Association
Mr. William H. Marten, III
Vice Adm. and Mrs. Edward Martin
Mathieson and Associates
Mr. Greg Mathieson
Lt. Jennah Mathieson
Adm. and Mrs. Henry Mauz

Capt. and Mrs. William McAree
Mrs. Carol McCain
Elizabeth McCance
Tidal McCoy
Siobhan McDonough
Mr. John McEnearney
Col. and Mrs. Joseph McGlinchey
Dr. and Mrs. John McMurdo
Mr. and Mrs. Corbin McNeill
The Medill School of Journalism
Mr. and Mrs. Tom Meurer
Mr. Robert Michael
Military.com and Mr. Chris Michel
Stephanie and John Miles
Gary Miller
Mr. and Mrs. Thomas Modly
Mr. and Mrs. Neal Moffett
Mrs. Chloe Moore
Capt. Ernest M. Moore Jr., USN (Ret.)
Meg Morgan
The Mullen Family Trust
Mr. and Mrs. Joseph B. Murphy
Dr. Michael Murphy
Catherine Murray
Lauren Murzinski
Vice Adm. and Mrs. Henry Mustin
Cdr. John Mustin, USNR
Maj. Gen. Mike Myatt, USMC (Ret.)

Alex and Staci Nathenson
National Museum of Naval Aviation
The National Museum of Patriotism
National Steel and Shipbuilding Company
Nauticus National Maritime Center
Naval Postgraduate School Foundation
Naval War College
Tee Nearman
Mr. Robert Newell
The Richard Nixon Library and Birthplace
Nomad Sound
Tanya Meurer Norman

Northrop Grumman Mission Systems Sector
Northrop Grumman Integrated Systems
    Sector

Mr. and Mrs. Philip Odeen
Orbital
Mr. David Orr

Mrs. Joann Palmer
Kate Patterson
Mr. Terry Paul
Katherine Paull
Mr. Ross Perot
Mr. Quang Pham
Mr. Thomas Philpott
The Photo Factory
Pirinate Consulting
Michele Predko
The Honorable Anthony Principi
Rear Adm. Bill Putnam, USN (Ret.)

Miss Elle Quinn
Mr. John R. Quinn
Mr. and Mrs. J. Thomas Quinn
QTC Medical Services

Sharon Rae
Mr. Michael Rafter
Allison Range
Jane Rauckhorst
RBX Industries
Mr. Lou Reda
Col. and Mrs. William A. Renner
Retired Officers' Association
Mr. George Rice
Dr. Mark E. Richards
Col. Albert F. Riggle, USAF
Mr. David Riordan
Risdon Photography
Mrs. Clark Ritchie
RKO Pictures and Mr. Ted Hartley
Mark Roberts

Mr. and Mrs. Frank Rocco
Sharon Roeder
Mr. Andrew Rosen
Mrs. Emily Rosen
Dr. and Mrs. Richard H. Rosen
Bradley Rossin
Rosemount Estate Wine
*Rowena's* Staff

SAIC
*San Diego Magazine*
San Diego Port District
Maj. and Mrs. Wesley Duane Schierman
Sedona Summit Resort
Sam Sewell
Mr. John Shaffer
Nancy Shaffer
Capt. and Mrs. Ned Shuman
Singular Sensations Catering
Mr. and Mrs. Carl Sloane
Alexandra Smith
Canda Smith
Mr. Frederick W. Smith
Nick Snyder
Square On Frames
Starbucks of Coronado
Mr. and Mrs. Ben Stevens
St. Stephen's and St. Agnes School
Aimee Strudwick
Mr. and Mrs. Alice Stuart
Lance Stuart
Blanca Soto
The Honorable and Mrs. Orson Swindle

Paul Tenney
Tent City Café
Capt. and Mrs. Frank Thorp
Tidewater Tidal WAVES
Time Life Foundation
TRW Foundation

Mr. Patrick Tucker

Dr. Harlan Ullman
Union League of Philadelphia
United States Naval Academy Alumni
    Association
Dr. Robert Ursano
USAA
Eduard Uzumeckis

Carla Vallone
Mr. and Mrs. Jorge Varela
Mr. and Mrs. Thomas Vecchiolla
Adrian Velazquez
Veterans of Foreign Wars
Veteran's History Project/Library
    of Congress

Kristi Walker
Mr. and Mrs. Jon Ward
Barbara Washburn
Casey Watson
Joanne Watson
Mr. George Watt
Mr. and Mrs. Rob Webster
Kristin Weikel
The Weikel Family Foundation
Ted Weinstein Literary Management
Capt. Kevin Wensing, USN
CWO David Williams, USA
Eric Wishnie
Ginger Wolstencroft

XL Associates

Mr. and Mrs. Peter Yates
Yavapai College Sedona Center for Arts
    & Technology

An extended thank you to all of our family and friends and the NAM-POW community who have stood by us through the development of *Open Doors: Vietnam POWs Thirty Years Later.* Your support and faith in the exhibit's creation is deeply appreciated.

## The Host Venues

Twenty venues around the country and overseas have hosted the museum exhibit *Open Doors: Vietnam POWs Thirty Years Later,* including:

Museum of History and Art
Coronado Historical Association

CHA's MoHA was the original host of *Open Doors* and has managed its nationwide (and overseas) tour. Its mission is to encourage and promote the appreciation, knowledge, and understanding of Coronado's unique art, architecture, history, and other historical resources. For more information, visit CHA's website at www.coronadohistory.org.

USS *Boxer* (LHD-4)

National Museum of Naval Aviation
Pensacola, Florida

Marines' Memorial Association
San Francisco, California

Hickam Air Force Base
Hawaii

Army Heritage Center Foundation
Carlisle, Pennsylvania

Free Library of Philadelphia
Philadelphia, Pennsylvania

Union League of Philadelphia
Philadelphia, Pennsylvania

Freedoms Foundation of Valley Forge
Valley Forge, Pennsylvania

The Richard Nixon Library and Birthplace
Yorba Linda, California

Nauticus
The National Maritime Museum
Norfolk, Virginia

U.S. Naval Academy
Annapolis, Maryland

The Stephen Decatur House Museum
Washington, D.C.

Naval War College
Newport, Rhode Island

Naval Postgraduate School
Monterey, California

National Museum of Patriotism
Atlanta, Georgia

Northwestern University
Medill School of Journalism
Evanston, Illinois

Yavapai College
Sedona Center for Arts and Technology
Sedona, Arizona

KAHA Art Gallery
Two Lovers Point, Tumon Bay, Guam
Sponsored by the Guam Chamber of
    Commerce

*Open Doors: Vietnam POWs Thirty Years Later* will be permanently housed, maintained, and displayed at the Library of Congress's Veterans History Project beginning in 2006. It will also still be available for temporary display at other venues upon request.

The Veterans History Project in the American Folklife Center at the Library of Congress is a national project created by the U.S. Congress in 2000 to collect and preserve the memories of veterans and those who served in support of the war effort during World War I, World War II, and the Korean, Vietnam, and Persian Gulf wars. The project works with more than 780 partner organizations across the country to collect and preserve veterans' oral histories as well as memoirs, photographs, letters, diaries, and maps. For more information, visit the project's web site at www.loc.gov/warstories.

*The* LIBRARY *of* CONGRESS
Washington, D.C.

VETERANS
HISTORY
PROJECT

# Psalm 139*

1 Lord, you have searched me out and known me; you know my sitting down and my rising up; you discern my thoughts from afar.

2 You trace my journeys and my resting-places and are acquainted with all my ways.

3 Indeed, there is not a word on my lips, but you, O Lord, know it altogether.

4 You press upon me and behind and before and lay your hand upon me.

5 Such knowledge is too wonderful for me; it is so high that I cannot attain to it.

6 Where can I go then from your Spirit? where can I feel from your presence?

22 Search me out, O God, and know my heart; try me and know my restless thoughts.

23 Look well whether there be any wickedness in me and lead me in the way that is everlasting.

*Some Biblical scholars believe this scripture was written by a Babylonian POW.

# Index

Numbers in *italics* indicate pages with photographs.

## A

Adm. Jeremiah Denton Foundation, 104
ages of POWs, 163
airplanes
    Blackjacks squadron, 77, 139
    commercial pilots (*see* commercial pilots)
    experimental airplanes, 76–77, 139
    gliders, 69, *70*
    shot down during Vietnam War, 154
*All That We Can Be* (Moskos and Butler), 154–55
Alvarez, Bryan, *92*
Alvarez, Everett, Jr., 4–6, *5*
    biographical information, 91–92
    boarding transport aircraft, *91*
    with family, *92*
    as first POW, 4, 153
    political interests, 158
Alvarez, Marc, *92*
Alvarez, Tammy, *92*
Alvarez and Associates, 92
Annapolis, Maryland, 78
Anshus, Richard C., 157
antiques and collectibles interests, 64–66, *65*
artistic interests, 58–60, *59*
aviators
    characteristics of, 1
    rank of, 154
    shot down during Vietnam War, 154

## B

Bailey, Lawrence R., Jr., 152
Baker, David E., 156, 161
"Be Prepared" (Lehrer), 81
Bean, James E., 156
Beekman, Brian, *93*
Beekman, Donna, 9, *94*
Beekman, Geneva, *94*
Beekman, Katy, *93*
Beekman, William D., 7–9, *8*

    biographical information, 93–94
    with mother, Geneva, *94*
Bethel Island, California, 64
Blackjacks squadron, 77, 139
Bliss, Ron, 28
Bolstad, Richard E., 156
books published by POWs, 161
    *Captive Warrior* (Johnson), 116
    *Chained Eagle* (Alvarez), 92
    *Code of Conduct* (Alvarez), 92
    *In Love and War* (Stockdale and Stockdale), 83, 146
    *Passing of the Night* (Risner), 138
    *Prisoner of War: Six Years in Hanoi* (McGrath), 59, 128
    *A Vietnam Experience: Ten Years of Reflection* (Stockdale), 146
    *When Hell Was in Session* (Denton), 104
Booz Allen Hamilton, 7, 93
Borling, John L., 160
Boy Scouts, 12, 16, 96
Boyd, Charles G., 160
Brace, Ernest C., 156
Breckner, William J., 160
Brenneman, Richard C., 156
Bring Paul Home campaign, 31
Brown, Charlie, 157
Browning, Ralph T., 161
Byrne, Ronald E., 156
Byrns, William G., 156

## C

Camilla, Georgia, 88
*Canberra*, USS, 34, 36
*Captive Warrior* (Johnson), 116
Cavaiani, Jon Robert, 155
*Chained Eagle* (Alvarez), 92
Cherry, Fred V., 156
Chesley, Larry, 158
Chile-Peru boder conflict, Vietnam POWs who served during, 156
Christian and Missionary Alliance (CMA), 160
civilians as prisoners, 165
*Code of Conduct* (Alvarez), 92
Coker, George T., 10–12, *11*
    on active duty, *96*

biographical information, 95–96
  with wife, Pam, *95, 96*
Coker, Pam, 10–12, *95, 96*
Collins, Donnie, 13–15
Collins, Thomas E., 13–15, *14*
  biographical information, 97
  political interests, 15, 158
  return of, *97*
Colorado Springs, Colorado, 58
commercial pilots
  John M. McGrath, 58
  Richard A. Stratton, 147
  Tony Marshall, 51, 121–22
  Wesley D. Schierman, 76, 139
communication between prisoners, 16–17,
  55, 72–73
Congressional Medal of Honor recipients, 155
*Constellation*, USS, 153
Conwal Inc., 5–6, 92
Cook, Donald G., 155
cooking interests, 52–54, *53*
Coronado, California, 146
Coronado Historical Association (CHA), 173
Crayton, Render, 16–18, *17*
  biographical information, 99
  with mother, *99*
  with son, Doug Crayton, *100*
  with wife, Fern Mackenzie, *100*

**D**
Dallas, Texas, 41
Daniels, Verlyne W., 156
Danville, Virginia, 45
Day, Doris, 19, 102
Day, George E. "Bud," 19–21, *20*
  biographical information, 101–2
  cockpit of 84-F, *101*
  at Col. Bud Day Field dedication, *102*
  Congressional Medal of Honor recipient,
    155
  with family, *102*
  Korean conflict service, 156
  World War II service, 156
Day and Meade, 19
Dayton, Ohio, 7–9, 61
demographics of casualties and POWs, 154–
  55

Denton, Jeremiah A., Jr., 22–24, *23*
  biographical information, 103–4
  as commandant of Armed Forces Staff
    College, *103*
  political interests, 22–23, 158
  promotion of, 160
  with Samuel R. Johnson, 40
  as U.S. Senator, *104*
Denton Program, 22–24, 103
Desert Storm, Vietnam POWs who served
  during, 156–157
dignity, fear of loss of, 1
divorce rates of POWs, 163–64
Dutton, Richard A., 156

**E**
education levels of POWs, 154, 163
Ellis, Jeffrey T., 161
Engaged Encounters, 96
Ensch, Becky, *105, 106*
Ensch, Beth, *105, 106*
Ensch, Chris, *105, 106*
Ensch, John C. "Jack," 25–27, *26*
  biographical information, 105–6
  running the Blue Angel marathon, *106*
  with family, *105, 106*
Ensch, Kathy, 25, *105, 106*
Ensch, Leon, 26
*Enterprise*, USS, 95
Epictetus, 84
escapes, successful and unsuccessful, 10, 12,
  152
experimental airplanes, 76–77, 139
eye surgeon, 43–45, 118, *118*

**F**
Fairbanks, Alaska, 143
faith, importance of, 1
federal contracting businesses, 5–6, 61
Fellowes, Cathy, *107*
Fellowes, John (son), *107*
Fellowes, John H., 28–30, *29*
  biographical information, 107
  with family, *107*
  promotion to captain, *108*
  reunion with wife, Pat, *108*
Fellowes, Pat, 28–30, *107, 108*

Fellowes, Sharon, *107*
Fellowes, Tom, 28–30, *107*
female POWs, 159–60
first POWs, 4, 152–53
Fleenor, Kenneth R., 161
Flynn, John Peter, 156, 160
Flynn, Robert J., 153
foreign nationals as prisoners, 165
Frederick, John W., 156
Freeman, Gayle, *118*
"Friends" (Hutton), 37
Fryett, George, 152
Fugitt, Alma, *114*
Fuller, Robert Byron, 160

G
Gaddis, Norman C., 156, 161
Galanti, Jamie, *110*
Galanti, Jeff, *110*
Galanti, Paul E., 31–33, *32*
    biographical information, 109–10
    with family, *110*
    *Life* magazine cover, *109*
    political interests, 31–33
Galanti, Phyllis, 31–33, *32, 110*
gardening interests
    Ben M. Pollard, 71
    Edward H. Martin, 52
    Thomas E. Collins, 13, *14*
    Tony Marshall, 51
Gartley, Markam, 158
*Gassed* (John Singer Sargent), 43
gliders, 69, *70*
Gough, James W., 156
Guarino, Lawrence N., 156
Guttersen, Laird, 156
Guy, Theodore W., 156

H
Hanoi Taxi, 157
Hanton, Thomas J., 156
Harrison, Jim, *150*
Hegdahl, Abe, *112*
Hegdahl, Douglas B., 34–36, *35*
    after capture, *111*
    biographical information, 111–12
    early release of, 36, 111

with James Stockdale, *112*
    welcome home parade, *112*
Hegdahl, Edith, *112*
helicopters shot down during Vietnam war,
    154
horses, 72
hot box, 47
humanitarian aid program, 22–24, 103–4
humanitarian medical missions, 44, *118*
Hutton, Eileen, 39
Hutton, James Hunter, *114*
Hutton, James L. "Duffy," 37–39, *38*
    biographical information, 113–14
    with grandson, *114*
    poetry interests, 37–39, 114
    return of, *113, 114*
Hutton, Mary, *114*

I
illnesses and injuries
    Ben M. Pollard, 69–71
    chronic pain and disabilities, 163
    John C. "Jack" Ensch, 25–27
    post-traumatic stress disorders (PTSDs),
        162–63
    while being held as POWs, 155
    William Beekman, 7–9
    William P. Lawrence, 47–48
*In Love and War* (Stockdale and Stockdale),
    83, 146
international aid program, 22–24, 103–4
International Voluntary Services (IVS), 159

J
Jenkins, Harry T., 156
John Paul II (pope), *123*
Johnson, Beverly, *115*
Johnson, Bob, *115*
Johnson, Ginie, *115*
Johnson, Samuel R., 40–42, *41*
    biographical information, 115–16
    on F-86, Shirley's Texas Tornado, *116*
    Korean conflict service, 156
    political interests, 40–42, 115, 158
    reunion with family, *115*
    with Shirley Johnson, *116*
Johnson, Sandra, 159

Johnson, Shirley, 42, *115, 116*

K
Kasler, James H., 156
Keep Our Promise to America's Retirees Act,
    102
Keirn, Richard P. "Pop," 156
Kernan, Joe, 158
Kientzler, Phillip A., 153
Kirk, Thomas H., 156
Kissinger, Henry, 31
Knights of Malta, 160
Korean conflict
    statistics on MIAs, 159
    Vietnam POWs who served during, 156
Kula, James D., 156
Kushner, Floyd Harold "Hal," 43–45, *44*
    biographical information, 117–18
    with Gayle Freeman, *118*
    humanitarian medical missions, 44, *118*
    return of, *117*
Kushner, Robert Lee, 45
Kushner, Robert Lee, Jr., 45

L
La Jolla, California, 16, 67
"The Lady of the Lake" (Scott), 47
LaGrange, Georgia, 16
Lamar, James L., 156
Larson, Gordon A., 156
last POWs, 153
Latendresse, Thomas B., 157
Latham, James D., 161
Lavin, Joe, *150*
Lawrence, Diane, *119*
Lawrence, Wendy, *120*, 120
Lawrence, William P., 46–48, *47*
    biographical information, 119–20
    with Diane Lawrence, *119*
    promotion of, 160
    at U.S. Naval Academy, *119*
Lee, Robert E., 31, 45
Lehrer, Tom, 81
Lehrman, Ronald J., 153
Library of Congress, Veterans History
    Project, 174
Ligon, Vernon P., 156

Little Padres Parks, 106
longest held POWs, 153
Lurie, Alan P., 161

M
Mackenzie, Fern, *100*
Marblehead, Massachusetts, 78
Marshall, Ann, *122*
Marshall, Maria, 51, *122*
Marshall, Tony, 49–51, *50*
    biographical information, 121–22
    with daughter, Maria, *122*
    with F-4D airplane, *121*
    with mother, Ann, *122*
Marshall, Veta, 51
Martin, Edward H., 52–54, *53*
    biographical information, 123–24
    with Pope John Paul II, *123*
    promotion of, 160
    with wife, Sherry, *124*
Martin, Sherry, 54, *124*
Maryland State Legislature liquor inspector,
    30
McCain, John S.
    biographical information, 125
    with Orson Swindle, 55–57, *56, 126*
    political interests, 55–57, 125, 158
    presidential campaign, 32, 109, 125
    return of, *125*
    with Ronald Reagan, *126*
McDow, Richard H., 157
McGrath, Jay, *128*
McGrath, John M., 58–60, *59*
    biographical information, 127–28
    with family, *128*
    POWs' facts and statistics, 165
    with wife, Marlene, *127, 128*
McGrath, Marlene, 58, *127, 128*
McGrath, Rick, *128*
McKnight, George
    with George Coker, 10, 12
    on Orson Swindle, 88–89
Mechenbier, Bernhard, *130*
Mechenbier, Edward J., 61–63, *62*
    biographical information, 129–30
    with family, *130*
    promotion of, 160

**179**

with Rick Webster, *129*
War on Terrorism service, 157
Mechenbier, Jerri, *130*
Mechenbier, Kari, *130*
Mechenbier, Mahli, 63, *130*
Mechenbier, Tai, *130*
medical benefits for military retirees, 19–20,
    21, 102
Meridian, Mississippi, 13
Merritt, Raymond J., 156
MIAs. *See* missing in action (MIA)
military retirees
    death rate, 21
    medical benefits for, 19–20, 21, 102
Miramar Air Show, San Diego, 61
missing in action (MIA)
    Hanoi Taxi to repatriate remains, 157
    statistics on, 159
Mobile, Alabama, 24
Mobley, Joseph S., 157, 160
model building, 11–12
Monlux, Harry, 158
Montagnards, 160
Moore, Chloe, 66, *131, 132*
Moore, Ernest M. "Mel," Jr., 64–66, *65*
    with Ben Pollard, 66, 69–70
    biographical information, 131
    with family, *131*
Moore, Leslie, *131*
Moore, Melissa, *131*
Moore, Michelle, *131*
Mullen, Jean, 67
Mullen, Peggy, 67–68, *68, 133, 134*
Mullen, Richard D. "Moon," 67–68, *68*
    biographical information, 133
    with Southwick and Stark, *134*
    with wife, Peggy, *133*
musical interests, 81–82, *82*, 143–44

N
NAM-POWs Inc.
    Congressional Medal of Honor recipients,
        155
    Hanoi Taxi, 157
    purpose of, 164–65
    website, 161, 165
Naval Aviation Cadet Choir, 81

Nelson, Marjorie, 159
*New Orleans*, USS, 131
*Nimitz*, USS, 95
Nixon, Richard, *138*
"No Man Is an Island" (Donne), 167
North, Kenneth W., 161

O
"Ode to a Porcelain Cup" (Hutton), 39
Olsen, Betty Ann, 160
Open Doors (museum exhibit)
    host venues, 173–74
    support for, 168–73
Operation Homecoming, 157

P
*Passing of the Night* (Risner), 138
*Paul Revere*, 131
Perot, Ross, 89
Peterson, Douglas, 158
philosophy interests, 84, 86–87
poetry interests
    James L. "Duffy" Hutton, 37–39, 114
    William P. Lawrence, 47–48
political interests
    Benjamin H. Purcell, 159
    Douglas Peterson, 158
    Everett Alvarez Jr., 158
    Everett C. Southwick, 159
    Harry Monlux, 158
    James Bond Stockdale, 146, 159
    James Shively, 159
    James Warner, 159
    Jeremiah A. Denton Jr., 22–23, 158
    Joe Kernan, 158
    John S. McCain, 55–57, 125, 158
    Larry Chesley, 158
    Leo Keith Thorsness, 159
    Markham Gartley, 158
    Orson G. Swindle III, 55–57, 89–90, 159
    Paul Galanti, 31–33
    Phyllis Galanti, 31–33
    POWs with public service careers, 157–
        59
    Ronald Webb, 159
    Samuel R. Johnson, 40–42, 115, 158
    Thomas E. Collins, 15, 158

Pollard, Ben M., 69–71, *70*
　　biographical information, 135–36
　　with family, *135*
　　homecoming of, *136*
　　with Mel Moore, 66, 69–70
Pollard, Ginny, *135*
Pollard, Joan, 66, 69, *135, 136*
Pollard, Mark, *135, 136*
Port, William D., 155
post-traumatic stress disorders (PTSDs),
　　162–63
Poway, California, 71
POWs
　　ages of, 163
　　books published by, 161
　　choices for, 2
　　demographics of, 154–55
　　divorce rates, 163–64
　　education levels, 154, 163
　　female POWs, 159–60
　　first POWs, 4, 152–53
　　how long they were held, 151
　　last POWs, 153
　　longest held, 153
　　number of POWs held, 151
　　number of POWs who died in camps, 151
　　professions of, 161
　　promotion of, 160–61
　　rank of, 153–54
　　service affiliation of POWs, 152
　　strength of, 2
　　support for other prisoners, 1, 16–17
　　treatment of, 2
　　where they were held, 151, 152
*Prisoner of War: Six Years in Hanoi*
　　(McGrath), 59, 127
professions of POWs, 161
Profilet, Leo T., 156
Project Mercury program, 46, 119
promotion of POWs, 160–61
Psalm 139, 175
PTSDs (post-traumatic stress disorders),
　　162–63
Pulma Labs Inc., 7–9, 94
Purcell, Benjamin H., 156, 158

Q
Quincy, Massachusetts, 85

R
Reagan, Ronald, *126*
Reynolds, Jon A., 161
Richmond, Virginia, 31
Risner, Dot, 72, 73, *73*, 138
Risner, Robinson, 72–74, *73*
　　after capture, *137*
　　biographical information, 137–38
　　Korean conflict service, 156
　　promotion of, 161
　　World War II service, 156
Rivers, Wendell B., 156
Robert E. Mitchell Center for Prisoner of
　　War Studies, 162
Rollins, David J., 156
Rutledge, Howard E., 156

S
SAIC (Science Applications International
　　Corporation), 61, 129–30
sailing interests, 78–80, *79*, 141–42
San Antonio, Texas, 73
San Diego, California
　　James L. "Duffy" Hutton, 39
　　Miramar Air Show, 61
　　San Diego Padres, 25, 27, 106
San Francisco Ceramics Circle, 64
Schierman, Alexa, *140*
Schierman, Cassie, 77, *140*
Schierman, Faye, *139, 140*
Schierman, Sandra, *140*
Schierman, Stacy, *140*
Schierman, Steven, *140*
Schierman, Steven (grandson), *140*
Schierman, Wendy, *140*
Schierman, Wesley D., 75–77, *76*
　　biographical information, 139
　　in F-89J aircraft, *140*
　　with family, *140*
　　with wife, Faye, *139*
Schwinn, Monika, 159
Science Applications International Corpora-
　　tion (SAIC), 61, 129–30
Scott, Sir Walter, 47–48
Sehorn, James E., 161
Shively, James, 158
Shumaker, Robert H., 161

Shuman, Dona, 78, *142*
Shuman, Edwin A., III, 78–80, *79*, 141–42
   with family, *142*
   with Nicholas Vanwagoner, *142*
Sijan, Lance P., 155
Simonet, Kenneth A., 156
Skelton, Red, 28
Smith, Phillip E., 153
Sooter, David W., 156
Southwick, C. Everett, 81–82, *82, 134*
   biographical information, 143–44
   as captain, *144*
   political interests, 159
   speaking engagement, *143*
   at the University of Washington, *144*
   in Vietnam, *144*
Spokane, Washington, 75
Stark, Bill, *134*
Sterling, Thomas J., 156
Stockdale, James Bond, 83–84
   biographical information, 145–46
   Congressional Medal of Honor recipients,
      155
   with Douglas B. Hegdahl, *112*
   political interests, 146, 159
   promotion of, 160
   with Robinson Risner, *146*
   with Samuel R. Johnson, 40
   with sons, *146*
   with wife, Sybil, *84, 145*
Stockdale, Jimmy, *146*
Stockdale, Sidney, *146*
Stockdale, Stanford, *146*
Stockdale, Sybil, 31, 83–84, *84*, 111, *145*,
   146
Stockdale, Taylor, *146*
Stockman, Harvey S., 156
Stratton, Alice, 87, 147, *148*
Stratton, Allyson, 85, *86*
Stratton, Amanda, 85, *86*
Stratton, Ashley, 85, *86*
Stratton, Charles, *148*
Stratton, Mary, 85
Stratton, Mike, *148*
Stratton, Pat, *148*
Stratton, Richard A., 85–87, *86*
   biographical information, 147–48

   on Douglas B. Hegdahl, 34, 36
   with family, *86, 148*
   homecoming of, *147*
Swindle, Orson G., III, 17, 88–90, *89*
   biographical information, 149–50
   with Jim Harrison and Joe Lavin, *150*
   with John McCain, 55–57, *56, 126*
   political interests, 55–57, 89–90, 159
   with Squadron VMF (AW) 235, *149*
   with wife, Angie, *150*

T
Tennessee state poem, 48
Terry, Ross, 60
Tester, Jerry A., 153
Thai (Pollard's dog), *135*
theology interests, 85–87
Thomas Aquinas, Saint, 87
Thompson, Floyd J., 153
Thorsness, Leo Keith, 155, 159
Thunderbirds, 40
Tonkin, Gulf of, 34, 153
TRANSFORM (Transportation for the Relief
   of Mankind), 104
Trautman, Konrad W., 156

U
United We Stand America, 149
Upper Marlboro, Maryland, 49
Urgent Fury, Vietnam POWs who served
   during, 157
U.S. Air Force
   airplanes shot down, 154
   POWs, 152
   values of, 61
U.S. Army
   helicopters shot down, 154
   POWs, 152
U.S. Marine Corp
   airplanes shot down, 154
   POWs, 152
U.S. Navy
   airplanes shot down, 154
   POWs, 152

V
Vegas, Camp, 46

Versace, Humbert Roque "Rocky," 155
Veterans History Project (Library of Con-
gress), 174
Vetter McCain (William Lawrence's dog), 46,
*47*, 48
*Victory* (ship model), 11
*A Vietnam Experience: Ten Years of Reflec-
tion* (Stockdale), 146
Vietnam War
combat casualty demographics, 154
MIAs, 157, 159
Vietti, Eleanor, 160

W
War on Terrorism, Vietnam POWs who
served during, 157
Warner, James, 159
Watertown, South Dakota, 34
Webb, Ronald, 159
Webster, Rick, *129*
*When Hell Was in Session* (Denton), 104
where POWs were held, 151, 152
White, Robert T., 153
Willey, Ed, 31
Williams, Angela, 149, *150*
Williams, Richard F., 156
Winn, David W., 161
Woods, Robert D., 156
Woos (the Moore's cat), *131*
World War II
statistics on MIAs, 159
Vietnam POWs who served during, 156
Wright-Patterson Air Force Base, 61, 62

# About the Authors

Jamie Howren was born in Washington, D.C., and raised in Alexandria, Virginia. She earned a bachelor of arts degree from Meredith College for Women in Raleigh, North Carolina, and spent a semester in Paris, France, studying under the direction of renowned fresco artist Ben Long. She also studied at the Maine Photographic Workshops in Rockport, Maine. Over the last fifteen years, Jamie has built a portrait business and created multiple portfolios focusing on landscapes and architecture. She has specifically created portfolios of Harvard Business School, Columbia University, and the U.S. Naval Academy. Jamie has worked worked several nonprofit organizations, including San Francisco-based Little Brothers—Friends of the Elderly and the Coronado Historical Association, donating her photography to their fundraising efforts. Since 2001, Jamie has dedicated herself to *Open Doors: Vietnam POWs Thirty Years Later* and is now working on a book for the U.S. Naval Academy and a portfolio of motorcycle images for a new exhibit. She lives in Rancho Santa Margarita, California, with her eight-year-old daughter.

Taylor Baldwin Kiland holds a master's degree from Northwestern University's Medill School of Journalism and a bachelor's degree in journalism from the University of Southern California. A former naval officer—the third generation in her family to serve—she has also worked as an account director for the global communications firm Burson-Marsteller and has volunteered for numerous national political campaigns, including Senator John McCain's in 2000. She continues to serve on several charitable boards of directors. Taylor's next two books, a children's book about careers in the Navy and a walking tour guide of the U.S. Naval Academy, will be published in 2006 and 2007, respectively. She lives in Arlington, Virginia.